THE SLUMS OF PALO ALTO

How to succeed through relentless failure

Mark L. Fussell

ISBN: 9862775-1-1
ISBN-13: 978-0-9862775-1-1

DEDICATION

Foremost, this book is dedicated to Rebecca: my love and my life; my partner and my wife. Rebecca was kind enough to stick it out through all my failures and all of our trials. She and I took this journey together, and through it grew to be better people.

During our journey, Maya and Katrina joined us. This book is dedicated to them too. They are amazing, and can make others more amazing by their presence and influence.

I thank my mother for nourishing me both physically and emotionally through both my younger and elder years.

And last, but not least, I thank M and V. Our life threads and karma waves are clearly connected in many ways, and knowing you both has made me a better person, and made this book a better book.

And to all the above: I enjoy and love you.
Thank you for being you and for being with me.

ACKNOWLEDGMENTS

This book is a miracle of generosity. To the many people that contributed to it, I can never repay you enough. I am amazed by what we have created together. A few of you were paid a trinket in dollars, but your contributions far exceeded that trinket. And most of you were paid either nothing at all or with a few stories from my heart. I thank you all: this product is yours. I hope you are proud of what we have created.

Editors
Anne, Art, Bill, Caden, Daniel, Eve, Geoffrey, Jeremy, Joe, John, Kathy, Katrina, Luis Jr., Maya, Penny, Rebecca, Roger, Ron, Steve, Timei, Jaya, Virginia, Xin Wen

Illustrators
Baird, Elizabeth

Photographers
Phoenix

Preproduction
Adrean, Bisrat, Hector, Justin, Karen, Karl, Mandi, Matt

Project Managers
Erin, Stephanie

CONTENTS

INTRODUCTION

The putting green on the balcony overlooked the Santa Monica pier. We were in the suite previously owned by Lawrence Welk, and could watch the taping of Baywatch[1] every Monday. During the day it was incredibly beautiful… it was the first of a series of too-beautiful-to-believe buildings that would affect my life. At night it was a bit scary. We were building a command center for a Saudi Arabian prince. Saudi princes have a lot of enemies, and when working late at night in our beautiful office it felt like all the enemies of our prince were figuring out ways to get to me. Rappel down from the balcony above? Sneak past the security cameras protecting the elevator? Apparently the prince was convinced by the Iraq war that CNN was a more reliable way to know what was going on around his country than other means, and he needed a command center that processed all this news to make sure he wasn't about to be overthrown or worse. I never heard the elevator pitch[2], but it could have been "Keep your neck with a palace of news".

This was the first of many startups that I was to be a part of. My story is not the story most people tell. The media talks about Facebook, Apple, Snapchat, and Google. Silicon valley is all about success: unicorns are everywhere and you just have to hop aboard one. Those stories may be true, but they are uncommon. And worse, those success stories usually gloss over the many sad aspects of each "win". Children abandoned. Spouses deserted. A life that is entertaining to others but shallow and meaningless to oneself. They are so doctored or simplified that they are unreal.

My story is a more common Silicon Valley startup experience. The real story. Only uncommon in its duration and perseverance. My family and I have ventured through a total of ten startups. Most people give up earlier.

---

[1] Baywatch: A television show about Los Angeles lifeguards

[2] Elevator Pitch: If you had to convince people to be interested in your company during a short elevator ride, what would you say? Maybe something like this "We are FaceLick dot com, like Facebook, but for pets! And all profits go to the SPCA"

Some other aspects are a bit uncommon too, but far more common than the pervasive unicorns. I am still happily married to my first love. And we have raised two daughters together. We are broke, but rich. We have been physically and mentally taxed for more than a decade, but are still thriving and in the best shape of our lives.

My family and I rent a house in Palo Alto. We are in the cheaper part of Palo Alto, where lawns are unkempt and foreign investors buy a house and leave it vacant year round. We are in the slums. Not because our house is inexpensive. It is worth approximately two million dollars. If you live in Palo Alto you commonly use single-digit or two-digit numbers to refer to house prices. The million is implied.

But our house is very poorly made: it is cold and hot on those rare days when Palo Alto is either cold or hot. We lose the phone and Internet connection on those rare days it rains in Palo Alto. And what makes us truly in the slums: on the first day of any month we could be evicted from our house for being unable to make the payment of five thousand dollars. My wife and two daughters on the street at a moments notice.

We are totally in the slums… it just happens that these slums are in the opulent heart of Silicon Valley. And the only way to get out is to progress… relentlessly…

ONE

My first startup was Third Point Systems or TPS for short. This was the summer of 1993 when the United States and other nations invaded Iraq. During this time the best information about the Iraq War was coming from CNN and other news stations. A Saudi Arabian prince had taken notice and decided he wanted a special command center to process all the news stations playing any kind of news, anywhere. A palace of news. That was our mission: to create a building and all the software necessary for it to be a command center watching over every news station, recording every minute of news, and enabling a team of analysts to distill it down for the prince.

When I interviewed with TPS they were in a tiny office in Pacific Palisades, but this project enabled them to move to Santa Monica, into what was previously Lawrence Welk's suite overlooking the Santa Monica pier. It was a beautiful office. We had a putting green on the balcony, we could look down and watch Bay Watch being filmed, and we could see when Cirque du Soleil came to town for the winter. We even overlooked the Shangri-La hotel where celebrities (maybe) frequently sun-bathed on the roof.

Being in a new office we had the standard debates on who should get what office space, but the office was huge and all the views were wonderful. So although there was a pecking order, the worst office was better than anything I had ever had before.

The head of development was previously a military developer, and possibly worked on Apache helicopters. The software team was responsible for building a flexible UI[3] control system that could enable all this video footage to be selected, processed, stored, retrieved, and distilled. Instead of simply building what was necessary to get the task done, the head of development wanted us to build something that could be configured to get *any* video processing job done and reconfigured on the fly. We were on a

---

[3] UI: User-Interface. The part of the computer and software that interacted with the user. Nowadays almost always graphical so UI and GUI (a graphical user-interface) are almost synonyms

classic path of excessive flexibility, which in the industry is commonly called "over engineering".

Along with building this meta-configuration[4] video pipeline processing system, I somehow gravitated into taking responsibility for all the office IT[5]. So I reviewed off-the-shelf[6] software that would help the TPS office run better along with reviewing off-the-shelf software that would help the palace. Being responsible for IT, it became obvious to me that it was far less intrusive if I did IT changes after everybody left for the day. That way I could test things out and make sure new software worked properly without impacting everyone in the office. So I started shifting my schedule to be more like 11AM to 9PM or even later. Given I was driving from Pasadena, this also helped reduce the commute time significantly.

Startups

I call TPS a "startup" but of all the startups that I will experience, it is the least clear that TPS matches the definition. To me, a startup must have aspirations (or delusions) of grandeur combined with an ability to fail. And by failing, I mean truly failing. To go bankrupt because there is not enough money for the vision to come true or even if it comes true, that vision is not valuable enough for a company to thrive. Some companies that are called successful "startups" actually succeeded because the pocketbooks of the founders were so large the "startup" could never have failed. These companies could continuously "pivot"[7] until things worked out. Small businesses like pizza shops are also not startups because they

---

[4] Meta-configuration: Meta is being 'about doing' something vs. 'actually doing' something. So this system was trying to be configurable in many different ways verses just trying to get something done

[5] IT: Information Technology. The software systems that run the company itself: email, document storage, a personnel database, and backups of all this data.

[6] Off-the-shelf: Software that you could simply buy in a retail store, or, nowadays, online at Amazon or a similar retailer. This is in contrast to custom built software, which costs quite a bit to develop and has high risks that it will never do what you want it to do

[7] Pivot: To change direction regarding what kind of product you are building, ideally based on having learned a lot more about your target market, and identifying a different and better problem to solve

have no delusions of grandeur: they simply want to have one or two or three successful stores.

Failure

I never failed anything before college. I might not have had the highest GPA in my school, or maybe I lost the top tennis position to a ringer, but I didn't fail. My family took academics very seriously. Whether instilled by my parents, sisters, schools, or what, we had a well-know grade system. An 'A' is an 'A'. A 'B+' is a 'C'. And a 'B-' is an 'F'. There might be exceptions provided for unusual peripheral classes, but for core curriculum that was the model. I don't think I ever failed anything with this grade system. Or if I did, I have blotted it from my memory.

Then I went to Caltech…

During the years I spent at Caltech we had 33% attrition. One in every three students simply didn't graduate from Caltech. Ever. Most of them wandered away after freshman year. A bunch more vanished after the first quarter of sophomore year. I couldn't have chosen any school other than Caltech after I was accepted, but it was a brutal education for most of us. They have changed "the catalog" quite a bit since then, so don't let my description dissuade you or your children from the school. Talk to a more recent graduate and let them dissuade you ☺

The reason for the sophomore exodus is that Caltech was Pass/Fail freshman year, so besides having possibly harder courses, sophomore first quarter is also the first graded quarter. I had a hard time with Caltech, but it wasn't the grades. I was quite ahead in math and a bit in physics, so I placed out of a total of three course-years of work. During freshman year I was taking a good number of sophomore level courses. And about the same number of freshman level courses. And I definitely learned how to fail. Big time.

Most fails don't actually become fails on your transcript, because you can see your trajectory and after a few weeks you can drop courses. So if you sign up for six courses, see the failures coming,

you can drop maybe two of the six and hunker down on the remaining four. If you went below four, you "went on the radar" of the undergraduate academic standards committee, and they might force you to take some time off. But if it only happened say once a year, they would probably let it slide. Back then, you were not allowed to go to Caltech part time.

Palo Alto

Palo Alto has many labeled neighborhoods. If you look at a Google map of the city, you will see them: Professorville, Old Palo Alto, Leland Manor, Triple El, and so on. I believe I count twenty-four of them. Palo Alto is twenty four square miles, so that works out to be a neighborhood for every square mile. Seemed a bit strange at first, but now it just *is*. We used to live in Leland Manor, Steve Jobs lived in Old Palo Alto, one of my daughter's friends lives in Downtown North, and we now live in St. Claire Gardens. The naming system is actually very convenient and a little more artistic than LA driving directions[8].

One • point two[9]

For Third Point Systems it wasn't clear what the grand scheme of the company was beyond the palace of news. The palace was quite grand on its own, but eventually we would finish it. We could have built many more, but how many palaces of news did the world really need? It also wasn't clear that TPS could ever fail. The prince's oil reserves could easily have funded us as a pet project forever. But I am going to give TPS the benefit of doubt and call it my first startup.

It was also the first and only company I have ever been *fired* from.

---

[8] LA driving directions are correctly spoofed on Saturday Night Live, and involve a turn-by-turn description of how to get somewhere, where "Take the 110 to the Santa Monica and exit on La Brea…" is amongst the shortest versions. Including traffic caveats and alternate routes is highly recommended…

[9] There is a meaning in this naming, that I will explain in more depth later. At the moment, please read this as "the second section about the topic 'One'"

My exit process started when one of the other employees told me how much he was being paid. I had my own self-image of how much I contributed to the company: I was smart, highly-skilled, and worked long hours building the core software system for TPS. In addition, I did *all* the IT work. But I was getting a fraction of one of my peers. I was not amused. So I wrote and left the CEO a note telling him how not amused I was and that I would like my salary adjusted. I left it for him late at night after the end of my standard shift.

The next morning, upon my arrival to our Lawrence Welk suite in Santa Monica, I was rapidly ushered into the CEOs office. The CEO told me that I must have looked at confidential payroll records to know another worker's salary. That my working a shifted schedule was causing havoc. And that my work in general was not acceptable. I was handed a termination letter, and I was walked to my desk to fetch belongings and then to my car. I drove home to Pasadena, mostly thinking, "*That wasn't worth the drive*".

Fini One

Love

Rebecca was sitting on the top bunk of a bunk bed when I first saw her. She was surrounded by "Flems". When I matriculated, Caltech[10] had seven houses. They were kind of like fraternities, but you were guaranteed to be in one of the seven. Each house had a proper name, and a nickname. Flems were part of Flemming. I ultimately became a Lloydie, or member of Lloyd. Rebecca was destined to become a Rudd as a member of Ruddock. But when I saw her sitting on the bunk we were both houseless. Caltech freshman go to Catalina Island as part of the assimilation process. We had taken a boat from LA and were now mostly-freshman in a Boy Scout camp on Catalina getting to know each other. We played a lot of Hearts[11].

[10] Caltech: The California Institute of Technology in Pasadena

[11] Hearts is a game where hearts are either very bad, or very good. If you win a few "tricks" with hearts, you would be penalized. If you "won" the queen of spades, you would be penalized thirteen-fold. But if you won all the hearts and

The ratio of men to women (or really boys to women) was 10:1 when I went to Caltech. In high school I had been exceptional academically, and fairly jockey athletically. I had three sports: Soccer, Swimming, and Tennis. Soccer I learned because I had to. Quaker schools played Soccer. If you are a boy and you don't play soccer, you are not a jock. A Quaker jock may sound like an oxymoron, but it definitely is not. Quakers may not believe in killing you, but they definitely believe in defeating you. I never made varsity soccer at my school, but every fall I gave it my all.

With a ratio of 10:1 you would frequently see ten-plus boys surrounding a single young woman. This was called "glomming" at Caltech, but I do not know if the word is officially defined. The boys wanted to be around the young woman. Most of them, myself included, had no idea what we were going to do if we were alone with the woman, but we still "hung out" around her. Orbited her. It was bizarre and natural at the same time.

As Rebecca will tell you, I was a confident (she would likely say arrogant) boy as a freshman. I was far more of a jock than most: I came to Caltech early for pre-season water polo. I had never played water polo in my life, but went through weeks of grueling practice, consumed whole pizzas at night, and was in the best shape of my life. Ultimately, I decided I did not like the foul play intrinsic to water polo. And I confidently simply quit and went on to better things. Like being with Rebecca ☺

But I am sure my confidence, athleticism, and intellect were not my killer weapons against the other glommers. I believe I had only three powerful weapons there: love, commitment, and a car.

Palo Alto: Community

Palo Alto has many labeled neighborhoods, but living in a labeled neighborhood does not create a community. You need people to

---

the queen of spades, you "shot the moon" and all those penalties would be bestowed on your opponents. Shooting the moon was quite a rush!

create communities. When we lived in Leland Manor we had Rebecca's[12] aunt two doors away, a very nice family diagonally opposite, and a couple more semi-social households. Our next-door neighbors were very quiet, either due to age on the one side or to the stresses of paying for a million dollar house on the other. Our neighborhood was not a community. It was not a community until one family, really one person, insisted that it should be. I will call her 'V'.

V moved to Palo Alto from San Francisco. Her parents live a couple towns north, in Atherton, but it seemed as though for most of her adult life, V wanted to be quite independent from them. V's family included a son the same age as Katrina[13], and later would include a daughter a bit younger. V was a firefighter. After her maternity leave had been fully exhausted, and the critical decision had to be made of whether to return to firefighting, she decided that the risk to her family was not worth the early retirement that this occupation provided. So V simply dropped the 'fire' off her occupation.

V and her family fought with the tiny house they were given, and turned it into house with a very nice layout, including an amazing kitchen and all the necessities for a tight family. V and her family fought with the yard, and now it is a farm with amazing vegetables, chickens, and a tree that Katrina can't keep her hands off. V fought to have the neighbors all know each other, and with yearly block parties and continuous social interaction, that ultimately became a reality. We had a community in Leland Manor, and V was the glue.

Love: Nature

Nature has an incredible influence on humans. Yosemite, the Grand Canyon, Bryce, Tahoe, Muir Woods, and many other natural wonders have heavily influenced my family and me. They are amazing. You need to see them. If you have a chance, put this book

[12] Rebecca is my companion of thirty years, and my wife of fifteen as of the writing of this book

[13] Katrina is my younger daughter

down right now and make the reservation. Then pick it back up: you can bring it with you.

Rebecca and I are especially enchanted by Yosemite. It is awesome, and its awe changes with the seasons, and with the shape of our family. Rebecca and I went several times when we were young. We have sat on the top of the fissures staring down several thousand feet at the beautiful valley floor beneath us. Today, just thinking about it, makes me shudder. I don't think at my current age I could sit there and look down. Too many images of accidentally "taking a leap" fly through my head.

Rebecca and I have also tried to hike up the mist trail to Nevada falls in the winter, but were ultimately repelled by snow and ice. And one Spring, our whole family caught giant snowflakes that poured down on us in a freakish April snowstorm. Yosemite is amazing. And so are all the other national treasures. Sometimes politicians do the right thing.

Startups: Right

Startups are trying to do as many important things right as they can before they run out of money. An important "right thing" is to have a singular visionary for the product. Products designed by committees do not do well. Sometimes two people are so mentally connected that together they envision better than a single person, but I have not really seen that. I have, however, seen layers of visionaries, with one big picture person and two or more details people, be quite successful.

It was not clear that TPS had a vision for selling many products, but TPS clearly had "the visionary" for the palace of news. I will call him 'F'. Besides being the overall visionary, 'F' was a fanatical documenter. He was at home with copious amounts of specifications. He produced copious amounts of specification. If I had a two or three sentence description of a feature for the palace, plus maybe a nice diagram, 'F' would send me back tomes of specifications with the words 'must', 'shall', 'may', and others with very rigorous definitions.

This kind of design is called a "waterfall": requirements in the form of documentation come pouring down from him, and the rest of us try to digest those requirements when he is done. We can't really build anything until he paints his vision enough. This approach is not ideal: generally the vision has to shift as the cost and feasibility of a requirement surface. But 'F' was used to the military way of doing things, so he was not pleased when prototypes of alternatives appeared. The alternatives worked well and were more feasible: a refinement to the vision. A dance with the details. Although I did not see the final product, if it ever existed, I am sure 'F' was not happy unless it matched his specification.

Startups: Wrong

Startups are trying to do many important things right, in time, but they are also trying to do nothing important wrong, at all. By 'wrong', I don't mean "not right". Startups can do many things that are not right until they run out of funding. By 'wrong', I mean things that will permanently damage the startup, making it unlikely to succeed at all.

Firing employees itself is neither right nor wrong… but firing employees for the wrong reasons is definitely wrong. Wrong for the startup. It produces a culture where people are scared of getting fired for arbitrary reasons. The CEO can write on a piece of paper that I did all these bad things, but coworkers are not going to believe a piece of paper. I spend all of my time with them. Over the history of my startups, very few CEOs spend much time with my coworkers at all.

Firing people for the right reason is very respectful to their coworkers. You are protecting them against the problem, verses asking them to "suck it in" and deal with the problem person. Later I would have to let people go for financial reason, which is unfortunate. But letting people go because they were a problem was difficult and rewarding at the same time. I knew I was helping the team at the cost of my suffering. I have to say, a few had such a bad attitude that I did not suffer at all.

Kindness

When Rebecca and I were still in Pasadena, we used to regularly eat Dim Sum on Sundays. Dim Sum is an extensive menu of snack-like Chinese dishes that are usually a single bite or two. The dishes can be made from fish, pork, chicken and other common (to most Americans) ingredients. They can also be made from tofu, intestines, chicken feet, and other less common ingredients. Many are 'dumplings' in a broad definition of the word: an ingredient wrapped by a noodle or similar starchy container. Kind of like ravioli, but imagine a hundred different variations with all kinds of interesting aspects.

Dim Sum is a lot of fun: you pick what you want from carts that wander a maze around the dining tables. Assuming you don't speak Cantonese, the servers are yelling lots of unfamiliar words: "Ha Gow", "Shao Mai", and so on. If you haven't had "Ha Gow", even recognizing the word isn't going to help you much. The servers get rewarded for you buying from them, so they will happily open the steamers to show you what is inside. That may or may not help you decide. Most newcomers to Dim Sum will pass on the chicken feet when they see it. But everything is edible and nothing is very expensive, so this is meant to test you willingness to try things. I promise you will enjoy at least one item at Dim Sum, possibly dozens of them.

One Sunday, Rebecca and I were having Dim Sum and a Caltech professor 'L' was there also. We knew 'L' pretty well, mostly because he was unusually nice. He was basically "just a professor" to us and not a friend or family member. But either intentionally or accidentally, he started me down the path to being unusually happy, having an enormous family, and trying to create a very different world from what most of us create for ourselves and others.

He stopped by our table about halfway through our meal. We talked a little bit, but no more than a couple minutes. And then he and his party left. Dim Sum is a very slow and enjoyable meal. You can't order most things; you have to wait until the cart that has the item you want comes by. Rebecca always wants (and now I always

want) a particular vegetable that is on a cart that is guaranteed to reach our table shortly before we would normally give up and leave. So finishing a Dim Sum meal could easily take us an hour and a half or more.

When we finally had finished, we gave the 'check' (a paper with a stamp for each item eaten) to a head waiter expecting to get back an actual bill. Strangely, nothing came back. So we tried again to pay our bill. But we couldn't. 'L' had paid it for us.

This may seem like a little thing. But it isn't. It is enormous. Both to you and for the person you are kind to. Whether a meal, a sincere complement, a computer, or your time, the act of gifting something you have to someone who might benefit from it, is the entrance to a very different world. A wonderful world.

A wonderful world I wanted to join.

TWO

I found startup number two shortly after finishing up with TPS and it was superior to TPS in almost every way possible. It was located in Pasadena, where Rebecca and I lived, so I could walk to it in less time than I could drive to TPS. The company was building products in the medical space, which is a little more socially responsible (IMO[14]) than protecting Saudi Princes. It had a CEO[15] that clearly understood the space his company was in, and clearly understood that he was running a start up. He appreciated that anybody who was willing to do what needs to be done should be considered valuable. The whole team was both very nice and very skilled. The view from the office was not quite as good as TPS[16] but it was still very nice and we could watch fireworks on the Fourth of July. And, finally, the software implementation language was Smalltalk, one of the greatest programming languages ever invented. The company was called Decision Support Group or DSG.

I loved DSG every single day I worked there. We created an Executive Information System (EIS) for hospital administrators, which showed them the financial and medical metrics they cared most about. The UI was made to look like the beautiful NeXT[17] UI; it was so beautiful that I printed all our UI widgets and laminated the paper. I still have that laminated card twenty years later.

Love: Programming

I am a professional programmer, which means I get paid to read and write software. Fortunately, I love to read and write software, so I am in the right business. Programming is amazingly powerful now

---

[14] IMO: In My Opinion. Or more formally In My Humble Opinion (IMHO)
[15] CEO: Chief Executive Officer. This is just a fancy name for 'President'. If you see paperwork for companies, 'President' is the dominant legal word, so the 'C'-prefixed title are really pomp
[16] Neither David Hasselhoff or Pamela Anderson were within telescopic view
[17] NeXT was the company that Steve Jobs founded after being ousted from Apple. It later became the basis of the modern Apple OSX UI, when Apple decided that Apple without Steve was not going to work

that robots, the Internet, and almost everything has some kind of program inside it. I started programming when programming was simpler, which made it easier for me to learn. And I am going to teach you how to program by going back to something similarly simple and even tangible.

For those who think they should scurry to the next chapter out of fear, please fear not. At worse I will fail. I am pretty good at that, but sometimes I don't. And for those who think they know the art of programming too well to stay, please don't scurry away, quite yet, either. For I am not going to just teach you how to program, I am going to teach you how to program in the only *true* programming language. This is not just a *great* programming language; it is truly what "The Matrix"[18] is made of. It is the language of the machines and the only true programming language to those machines. It is named "Machine Language". Sadly, computer people are commonly very rigorous and not very creative about how they name things.

To learn the one true language, you will need some playing cards and a desk or relatively empty space in which to work.

Now take the deck of cards you have and remove all the eights, nines, tens, jacks, and kings from it. You are left with ace through seven plus the queens. Why the queens? Because women are awesome! But also, a 'Q' looks a lot like a '0' if you squint hard enough. So please squint a bit and you will now have the digits from 0 through 7 as cards in front of you.

Some computer terms may already be familiar to you. A 'bit' is a binary digit: either '1' or '0', either true or false. A 'byte' is eight bits and can represent any number from '0' through '255'. Well, four 'bits' or half a 'byte' is a 'nibble' and can represent the numbers from '0' through '7'. Computer people, if they let their hair down, can actually be creatively whimsical at times too ☺

---

[18] "The Matrix" – 1999 by The Wachowski Brothers, Joel Silver, and Warner Bros.

Community: Education

At approximately the same time that V glued together our proximate neighbors, we were becoming an integral part of another community. Maya was now almost three, and somehow Rebecca had heard of a place called Parents Nursery School (PNS). This was just a couple months after we moved to Palo Alto, but we were already rapidly becoming a part of PNS's incredibly strong community. When Rebecca and I were looking for nursery schools, we saw a number of different variations. Some were clean and pleasant, some were clean and almost industrial, some were a bit more disorganized, and then there was PNS. PNS was a fantastic battleground. On this battleground there was a war between Kids allied with Nature against Adults trying to produce Order. Every day the kids were clearly winning: they were having a marvelous time, and only obeying a few critical rules. And the adults were happy to see it, if a bit frazzled trying to keep the children alive.

Where as "modern" playgrounds have nice rubber surfaces, PNS simply put tires on top of the concrete 'curb' that surrounded the play structures. Where most schools tried to protect their flora, the kids at PNS would constantly be bouncing on the trees and running through the ivy. At PNS, kids were free to be kids, as long as they did not hurt each other, as long as they included each other in their activities ("you can't say you can't play"), and as long as they at least approximately did what the teacher and parents said they should do.

PNS was a cooperative. Parents were formally "in school" learning how to teach children. Parents also had to attend mandatory nighttime classes, but the bulk of the time was spent in school with the kids. Rebecca was the primary time-contributor to all our cooperative schooling, but when Maya went through PNS, I was there fairly often too. Sometimes I was there in the main part of the school day, but more likely during working weekends. One year I drew all different kinds of smiley faces on the playground tires when I re-holed them. The holes were to let water drain, and the faces showed 'up'. Another time I helped rebuild a water table. And another time I dug a hundred holes to stash buried treasures for the kids to find. PNS was a lot of fun, and was definitely an important

community to us.

Failure • point two

I failed courses at Caltech for all kinds of reasons. Sometimes the material was insanely hard. I always had bad study habits. I won the 10:1[19] odds and had an amazing woman that I wanted to be with. And sometimes I had bad karma.

The worst karma I ever had back then was in a VLSI[20] course. The scale has changed, and the layers are different, but if you look at a current computer's CPU[21]… that is VLSI. I don't know if the chip industry has augmented the name as things have become more and more complex. In any case, I *absolutely loved* VLSI. It combines building electronic circuits with graphic design. I loved both of these: I even took a year off from Caltech to study graphic design at UCLA.

As part of the VLSI course, there was a contest. Who can build the smallest "Full adder". A full adder can handle adding a binary digit to another binary digit, including the carries in (from the right) and out (to the left). So if nothing is coming in from the right, '0' + '1' = '1' with no carry, and '1' + '1' = '0' with a carry of '1' to the next digit to the left. This is how computers add numbers, which are represented in Base-2 (just '1's and '0's).

I loved this contest. I relished the chance to prove I had the graphical skill to lay out this relatively simple circuit in the smallest space possible. VLSI circuits have multiple layers, and transistors are kind of like traffic lights, so this challenge was akin to laying out a three-dimensional set of intersections with the tightest road density possible. Manhattan on steroids.

I loved the challenge and put many extra hours into it. Finally,

---

[19] 10:1 is a Ten-to-One ratio. Ten men to one woman

[20] VLSI: Very Large Scale Integration. The making of computer chips

[21] CPU: Central Processing Unit. The core functionality of a computer although the graphics chips are very important now too

we all submitted our homework, and the professor or TAs[22] reviewed it all. During our next class, the professor shows a slide that has the geometric outlines of all the different solutions. Lots of squares and rectangles inside one another with the smallest in the center. It is hard to be sure the scale, and squares are not a very distinct object, but I hope I am near the center.

Next the professor calls my name. He tells everyone that I have the smallest design, by a large margin actually. But. It doesn't work. My smallest square has a thin line around it. It needs a thick line. That shows it works. Mine doesn't.

Testing VLSI in the 1980s is not very easy. The tools we students are using can't simply run the electronics. What we are using are basically drawing tools. So I drew a three dimensional picture in a square that was supposed to work as a circuit, but the professor or TAs claim it does not. I don't know if they had the tools to check it. Or they eyeballed something that I couldn't see.

Later I go see the professor. I ask if he can explain what is wrong with my solution. I really can't figure out the problem. He tells me to go figure it out myself.

He was not the nicest professor at Caltech.

Education: Boxes

I was at a company meeting for one of my "middle" startups, and the CEO was running various teamwork games. There were maybe thirty of us, and the current game was for each of us to find out three interesting things about every other person there. So if you stayed "in the box", each of us had to interview thirty other people. And I think we had five minutes within which to do it in. Given the impossibility of this task, the CEO asked for strategies to accomplish it.

---

[22] TA: Teaching Assistant. Caltech did not have a lot of these because the student to faculty ratio was 3:1, but some professors did have TAs. This one had several

A few people mentioned different approaches, and then I suggested "Why don't we each write down what is interesting about ourselves, and then we can just copy it thirty times (say pass the sheets around in a circle) or just accept that we have clearly achieved the result?" This was a strategy that would take about five seconds to achieve the desired outcome. Or at worse a couple minutes if we really needed to do a bunch of copying. Seemed obvious. At least to me.

The CEO asked everyone if they wanted to do it that way. There was a strong majority who said no. They liked the artificial, restrictive, box of having to interact individually with everyone. Even when the box was made visible to them. Even when they knew, deep down, that their box could make them fail. Maybe their box felt like Temple Grandin's Hug Machine[23], and they couldn't give that up.

So we wasted five minutes doing nine hundred interviews. Or more like fifteen minutes after a couple extensions for time. Or maybe it was slightly fewer interviews due to some minor benefit of a different approach. I don't remember. I do remember that everyone failed to interview someone, and I believe no one else remembered to interview the CEO himself, so collectively we all failed the game. Together. In our "happy box".

Two • point two

We also had a fantastic graphing package from a highly skilled Smalltalker who lived in Santa Cruz. An amazing thing about Smalltalk is that you can see everything: all the code from the operating system upward through the development tools is visible to any programmer. So you could learn from all the great minds that built these things. If you were a decent programmer before going into Smalltalk, you could become a legend if you just learned from all that you could see.

---

[23] Hug Machine: A machine that hugs you like a person would (deep surrounding pressure) but removes the human-interaction from the equation

So DSG was a dream, but I am not there anymore. What gives? DSG "exited". DSG's corporate vision was to get networks of hospitals using our software. But DSG ran out of money, and the founders successfully sold it to a company on the East Coast. We had a period of due diligence, and then the sale went through. In spite of being at DSG for less than a year, the president gave me a significant bonus. Very classy.

While at DSG, I also came up with the right way to negotiate salary with any sane employer. I am not sure it would have worked with TPS, but the approach is very simple. Accumulate a collection of "This is what I did for you" descriptions. Then say "I believe that is at least equal to what this person is doing for you". Finally "I would like to be compensated equivalently". Voila. A sane boss will do exactly that. I had this exact conversation about a month into working for DSG and the salary was adjusted immediately. Again, *very classy*. I used DSG and its very classy CEO as my model when I launched my own startup. I ultimately lost a lot of money as CEO, but I believe I maintained a lot of class.

When DSG was being sold, Rebecca moved to San Francisco to work for OOCL[24]. We were in a long-distance relationship for a couple months, but DSG moved to Vermont after the sale. I could have moved there too, but found Rebecca and San Francisco more compelling.

Fini Two

Love: Family – Horses, Dragons, and Rams

Our household is of both Western and Eastern decent, so our family has two zodiacs that we know quite well. The Western zodiac says Rebecca, Maya[25], Katrina, and I are a ram, two scorpions, and a bull. Those symbols do not really fit our personalities at all.

On the other hand, the Eastern zodiac says I am a fire horse.

---

24 OOCL: Orient Overseas Container Lines. A major shipping company

25 Maya is my first-born daughter, and Katrina followed her three years later

That totally fits: I was running full speed, blazing over the hills of eastern America. I felt like something totally alien to my habitat there. I was having fun, but I didn't belong there. Then I came to California, and on a brief visit to Catalina, I saw, on the top bunk, another fire horse. Rebecca. And from that point forward I wanted to run with her. We have been running side-by-side for thirty years.

Maya is a golden dragon. That totally fits too. Maya is amazing. She is very quiet while being very social. She has great humility while having incredible confidence and talents. She is a hidden dragon. She looks like a young woman, but she could conquer the world. Fortunately she seems to be a very friendly and good dragon.

Katrina is a water ram. That *totally* fits. Katrina is also amazing, but the first thing you will encounter about her is a butting of heads. Hard. Like she wants to bonk you into unconsciousness with her intellectual power. Katrina could also conquer the world, so we are working very hard to make sure she is a well-adjusted young woman who seeks to do good things. Otherwise, we all better get out of here.

Slums

To be perfectly clear, I am not claiming that Palo Alto has parts of it that are like the slums of Rio De Janeiro or Kolkata. At worse, we have (or had) a trailer park, which was probably much safer and cleaner than the next town over. And we have a strange part of Palo Alto where the residents do not go to the Palo Alto unified school district. But Mountain View is a perfectly good school district, and people like Salman Khan and Rebecca's cousin are making it better by the day.

By *slums* I mean a place where (a) people are experiencing an *appreciably worse* standard of living than those around them, (b) those people have *no economic power* to make their lives significantly better without emigrating, (c) people's health and happiness are *meaningfully impacted*, and (d) there is *imminent threat of things getting much worse.*

If my definition of '*slums*' is so irreconcilable with your own that

you must stop reading, I understand. If you have not bought the book yet, please put it back on the shelf. If you already own it, it may be a good white elephant gift.

If you are still here: Rebecca and I did not actually move into the slums. They came to us.

Rebecca, Maya, and I lived in a two-story apartment in Sunnyvale that we called *the castle*. It was one of the show apartments for the apartment complex, so it was larger than most and located much better than any other. Our apartment was on the third and top floors, had huge windows facing south and west, and projected up and outward in ways that made it look like a turreted tower. Rebecca and I had our bedroom on the top, and Maya and I shared "my office" on the bottom. We had enough space for three, but it was very cozy. Before we moved to Palo Alto, Rebecca was pregnant with Katrina. Four of us would be a bit too cozy for our castle.

We moved to Palo Alto because Rebecca found a nice house for rent two doors away from her sixth Shen aunt. When Maya saw the place, she loved that the layout was circular: you could go from the front to the back in two ways, and she ran round and round that circle pretty much the whole time we viewed the house. The house had three real bedrooms, and two real baths, but the new owners had somehow managed to drop another room and bathroom into the garage. We weren't sure this was legal, but it made a good office space.

The rent for the house when we moved in was not appreciably more than the apartment, and I was working full time for the "Big Evant" as a well-paid W2 employee, so the financial numbers were fine. It was a very exciting time for Rebecca, Maya, and me. And Katrina would grow to love that house very dearly.

Right: Culture

Building the culture of a startup is a critical task. DSG had done a great job of making people feel a part of the company and responsible for getting things done. We were a team with different

skills, different backgrounds, and different roles, but we were all trying to build a high-quality and useful product.

I am not sure how the president and his top aids managed to get this team. I came in too late to see it form. I just know I felt a welcomed addition and worked very well with my coworkers. I had no desire to leave DSG, so I was saddened when it left me and moved to Vermont. A couple employees would try to go with it, but the transition from California to Vermont is a bit too harsh, and they returned after the first winter.

Wrong: Timing

I was not very informed about DSGs timing: how long it had been around, how much money it had initially, why it "ran out of time". I was just a programmer and wanted to work in this fantastic culture, in the amazing programming language we used, building a very cool product, and getting paid for it as well. Nirvana. And blissful ignorance. Timing turned out to matter for almost every startup I was to be a part of. One lost all its potentials because of 9-11. If that had been 11-11 instead, it might have closed all the deals before the fateful day. Another hired so many people that it ran out of money years before it should have. Time is among the most critical aspect to a startup. Not enough time, and you can't find and delight your customers. Too much time, and you are not hungry and focused. Too much time, and something bad can happen. Too little time, and you can't recover.

There is no guaranteed solution, but after ten startups, I recommend trying to travel rapidly, in the right direction, with the least amount of fuel (money) possible. Being stingy with fuel will make the process take longer, but it is more likely you can stay in the race through a decent exit (the ultimate finish line for a startup). Even with some unlucky timing.

Kindness: Wedding Wine

Rebecca and I were together for fifteen years before we go married.

We call it "The French Model", where you get married to have children. It was also kind of nice to get married the same millennium as we first met, and it was now the year 1999. Invitations in both English and Chinese went out early in the year, and the celebration itself was on July Second (a Friday) so people would have a long weekend to enjoy San Francisco and Monterey.

Rebecca and I were both working at fairly well-paying jobs, had no expensive hobbies, lived in a modest apartment, and had no children, so we had quite a bit of money we could spend on a once-in-a-lifetime party. We rented a mansion in the hills, rented all the normal wedding/party supplies like golden tables and chairs, hired a photographer, and had a catered dinner with several different entrees. That was our "normal" party.

Rebecca and I are not normal, and this was not meant to be a normal party. Rebecca and I care too much about many things to be normal. And we have family and friends that make it possible for us to be even less normal than even we can imagine.

Our wedding music was provided by Rebecca's sixteen year old cousin who plays the French horn beautifully and organized an ensemble for us. We flew in cheese from France, Switzerland, Italy, and other parts of the world. We flew in fruit from Asia. We bought hundreds of Lego Sets and Beanie Babies to be party favors and to help people meet each other. And instead of a singular wedding cake, we had eight different ones.

This was meant to be a wonderful celebration and feast. Almost a hundred of our friends and a hundred of Rebecca's family showed up to celebrate with us. Strangely, only three of my family members participated. To this day, I can't imagine what they were thinking. For beside all the wonderful items described above, there was one more.

Wine! And by wine, I mean wines amongst the best you could savor anywhere. Wines acquired directly from the vintner by the case, stored properly in cooled cellars, and opened just as they had aged to full body. Wines spanning a decade of different stellar

vintages. Wines that our guests still rave about years later. Quite possibly worth more than all the other parts of our feast. I am not sure, because I did not buy them.

It was a gift. From 'B' and 'L'

UNION SQUARE PLAZA HOTEL
LEMONADE. UPGRADE
UNION SQUARE PLAZA
Mason

THREE

I worked as a contractor and consultant for several years, and then stopped working shortly before my first daughter was born. About a year and a half later, a friend and coworker asked me if I could help them out. The company was Evant, earlier named Retail Aspect.

Evant was in the process of landing[26] Staples with their product: a retail planning application. If you take a retailer like The Gap, they have to plan what clothes they will have in the store for each month of the year. They can use previous years to help their predictions, but each year new styles and colors come out, so it is somewhat a mystic art to figure out what customers will want and get the store inventories right. Planning tools help the company's planners work with huge amounts of historical data, huge numbers of stores, and huge number of items. The planners want quick responses as they transform the plans for the entire fleet of stores.

I forget what Staples store count was, but The Gap has about two thousand stores, so Staples is probably similar. Two thousand stores, maybe a thousand products, diverse variations on the products, and planning at the day or week level. For each product there could be several dozen metrics. And we also have several years worth of historical data at the item level. So in total the planning application has to work with billions of data points... *at the least.*

Staples loved the Evant product. Very leading edge UI, flexible planning engine capabilities, apparently very fast, and so on. Great features that would help Staples' planners work more effectively compared to what they were doing already. Looked good to go forward into actual production use. Except for a "little problem". The planning application was a prototype: it was written to work and look good. But it had not been built to deal with a billion data points. And, to make things worse, it had been written by someone who was no longer with the company. So my friend made a very simple request: could I turn this complex prototype into the real thing? In

---

[26] Getting a large company to purchase a lot of your product, just like catching the big fish in a lake

three months or less?

Startups: Coffee

I did not drink coffee at all until after college. At some point after that, Rebecca and I found a great bakery and coffee shop on the edge of what became the shopping section of Pasadena called "Old Pasadena". Originally this section of town was *very seedy*, and even during its gentrification, certain kinds of stores (the kind that Rebecca and I would be unlikely to frequent) stayed in business an amazingly long time. The great bakery was at the end, was nice and airy, and looked out over the gorge that now holds the 710. They served coffee in bowls. It was very good, and I might partake in a mocha once a week.

When Rebecca and I moved north to San Francisco and joined OOCL to work on a large Smalltalk[27] project, I think I started drinking a bit more coffee. I think it was a sporadic ritual, and I know I was a lightweight in the coffee arena. One day before work, I went to a new coffee shop that does two shots of espresso in their mochas by default. I was *wired* that day, and made sure to call the number of shots (1) in the future.

The Evant project changed all that. I had been home with Rebecca and Maya for at least eighteen months. I mountain-biked several times a week, up some serious mountains. I had plenty of money in the bank, so I didn't need to work at all… at least for a while longer. I liked my life.

I also liked the Evant challenge laid before me. "Could I turn this complex multi-dimensional prototype into the real thing? In three months or less?". That was a great challenge. In addition, the Evant team had several of my friends in it: at least two were at my wedding. And the new Evant people I met, I immediately liked them too. I wanted *both lives. Concurrently.*

Turns out, you can do that. You simply multi-task at some

---

[27] Smalltalk is a computer programming language, which I will discuss a bit later

proper unit of granularity. I picked by the day. Monday, Wednesday, and Friday: I would go into Evant and work my butt off. The other four days I kept for my family life. These other days, I might respond to an email or do some amount of work at home, but I was definitely not *at work*.

To get what Evant needed to be done, actually done in three months or less, was not a part-time task. It was a normal 40+ hours a week kind of task. So I worked twelve to fourteen hours each day that I went in to Evant. Arrived around 7AM. Left at 9PM. Rarely had lunch. Really only consumed one kind of food.

There was a Starbucks on the ground floor of the Evant building.

I am no longer a lightweight.

Family: Homes

When I was growing up, I lived in a single house the whole time. So naturally I called it my home. Even when I went to boarding school, that did not change my home. Unlike Harry Potter, for me school was school and home was my parent's house. I would go to school and return home. We would vacation in Cape Cod or Bermuda, and then return home.

When I went to college and found the love of my life, the definition of 'home' became very confusing. My classic 'home' was my parent's house. But when I went there one winter without Rebecca, it was clearly not where I wanted to be. I wanted to be with her, or I was not in any kind of 'home' at all. But at Caltech people commonly shifted dormitory rooms every year, and for quite some time Rebecca and I did not share an apartment. That would have to wait until after my epic failure. So my 'home' could no longer be attached to any place. I could either view myself as homeless or revise my definition of 'home'. I did the latter, and for 30 years, my definition of 'home' is simple: it is being with Rebecca. If I am with her, whether in Palo Alto or Bangalore, in a car or a plane, awake or asleep, then I am home.

Failure: Most Epic

My most epic failure was also my fastest. It took only a minute or two. And it was twenty five years ago, in 1989. Going back to that fateful evening…

Tonight, Rebecca and I are having dinner with our families. It is the night before we formally walk: tomorrow we get a nice piece of paper for graduating from Caltech. Graduating from Caltech has not been easy for either of us, so this is a very significant event. And having most of our family around us is really nice too. We are incredibly happy.

Rebecca has a cat named Houdini. She found Houdini as a stray, washed her up, and out popped a beautiful Norwegian Forest cat. Houdini is amazingly smart and quite friendly too. Amongst the best cats I have ever had or seen. Houdini got her name "Harriet Houdini" based on her ability to escape from closed rooms. During the recent school year, a friend was staying in a house near Caltech, and Rebecca sometimes kept the cat at that person's house. During the day, Houdini would be safely locked in a room with closed windows and a closed door, but by afternoon she would magically escape and appear outside the house wandering the yard. This happened many times. The friend swore he did not let her out. Hence the name[28].

But tonight, Houdini is staying in Rebecca's mother's condo in Chino, about forty minutes east of Pasadena. Rebecca has been staying in that condo for maybe half a year or so, and given Houdini is there, Rebecca has to go back there to feed her. Most of Rebecca's clothes are there too, so she needs to go back to change as well. So after dinner, Rebecca, the love of my life, departs to Chino.

An hour or two later I get a call from Rebecca. It is maybe 11PM or midnight, the night before our graduation. I am a night owl[29], so I am awake, but I am definitely surprised by the call. Rebecca says something like "Can you come and get me?" She may also say, "I am in the hospital", but I am not sure. Later in my life, I will know the right answer to this very simple question, but the two-minute epic failure of my life involves me saying things like "What are you talking about?", "You are an hour away!", and "It is graduation night!". The only right answer is: "Yes, I will be right there!" Not saying those six

---

[28] Decades later the friend recanted. He has a quirky sense of humor

[29] Night Owl: A person who frequently stays up beyond midnight

simple words immediately will forever be my life's crowning failure.

Rebecca had been assaulted at knifepoint in her Chino condo's carport. Whether the person wanted just money or something worse, we will never know. Rebecca screamed and amazingly grabbed the knife. By the blade! Fortunately this reaction scared the perpetrator off. A call to 911 and Rebecca was escorted by police to the hospital.

She is calling me from there. After having survived a mugging at knifepoint. While I complain about the hour-long drive before me. Again, my life's crowning failure. And one I immediately committed to never even getting close to again. To never fail her *again.*

We walked and formally graduated the next day. Rebecca's finger is bandaged to protect the deep wound and its stitching. We are both very tired, but very happy.

We have rarely been apart since then. It is now twenty five years later.

Programming • point two

Now that you have lots of nibbles to play with, you need to define the rules of your card game. *You* are the machine. This is *your* language, so you can pretty much do whatever you want except: (a) you must obey your language, and be able to explain your language to anyone (e.g. "me"), and enable me or anyone else to become just like you, (b) you currently can only work on the table, and (c) you currently can not overlap cards, so your workspace is flat (one layer). And if you are younger than eighteen or are seriously unboxed: no writing on the cards, tearing up the cards, flipping the cards over, making card houses from the cards, gluing the cards to various other objects, and so on. Oh and finally, you cannot react to the suit of the cards. You can have any number of decks and suits, but all queens are identically '0'.

If you need an example to kick you off, put three cards down: 'A', '2', '3' where the 'A' is a '1' but that won't matter in this case. For *my language*, I want an 'A/1' to mean "Add the next two nibbles".

So this sequence is telling me to add '2' to '3' and that gives me '5'. To keep things simple, I will put the answer as the next card. So if given the input 'A23' I should change the state of my desk to 'A235'. Hurray! You and I have now learned my Machine Language. You can now program *me* ☺

So knowing just this single instruction, you should be able to respond to 'AQQ' ('AQQQ'), 'A34', and 'A3Q'. Am I correct?

How about 'A45'?

Three • point two

Turning a prototype into a real product is real work. A good prototype does the right things in the wrong way. A phrase I will attribute to Kent Beck and the Unix culture in general is:

- Make It Work
- Make It Right
- Make It Fast

A software prototype focuses solely on the first item. A good prototype nails the "It Works". A smoke and mirrors prototype fakes even that.

Evant had a good prototype when I arrived. The code clearly "worked" for the scenarios put in front of it. And there were dozens of "Customer Tests" that proved that it worked for those scenarios. "Customer Tests" are test-runs of the entire system that a customer (sometimes called a 'user') can understand in their own terms[30], and that they could verify that the resulting answer was correct. A Customer Test would not necessarily have to interact with the UI, but it should show the core behavior of the system "knows how to make the customer happy". So '2+3' should equal '5'. The Evant prototype passed all these customer tests to date, so I primarily needed to deal with the next two bullets. I had to:

---

[30] For example, I want to add 2 to 3 and see what the result is

- Make It Right
- Make It Fast

These are things I excelled at. My talents combined with caffeine would completely throw away the old code base and produce a new one that was blazingly fast and organizationally correct. And it would pass all the existing automated customer tests plus dozens (eventually hundreds, then thousands) of new ones. Ultimately we had both an incredible suite of tests proving everything worked correctly and an incredible suite of benchmarking tests that proved everything worked quickly. Break something about the code base, and alarms would go off. Regression was not an option.

Education: Chakras

My family and I spend an enormous amount of time and money on education. It is somewhat focused on our own children, but our efforts and time spill out into the larger community. I run a free robotics club called PaloBots that my daughters participate in, but most of the club is filled with other people's children. Rebecca helps out in the classrooms of Ohlone, and our daughters benefit from this, but so do a couple dozen other kids. We invest in children because we care about children. We are trying to help them succeed, be happy, and be resilient enough to thrive against the hardships of the world.

As our daughters and their peers became older, we started giving them more freedom and authority. They now needed to interact with the world directly. To stand up for themselves. To express their needs to others, and graciously accept the gifts others give to them. Within the last couple of years, I have started viewing this 'assertiveness' as among the most critical things my daughters needed to learn. They were academically successful, athletically active, and socially responsible. But they were timid, and needed to become assertive for their own and other people's benefit. I think my daughters are on the right path and making reasonable progress. They are doing fine.

But other kids are not, so I hope people reading this passage will

consider what they can do to help. I call it unblocking children's chakras. Because some of them have seriously blocked chakras. And however smart or not, sweet or not, happy or not they are, if they don't unblock certain chakras around asking for and receiving help, they are doomed. I am not sure what they are doomed to exactly, but I am quite sure it will not be a happy life.

My wife's family is very large. Her father had two brothers and six sisters. Chinese almost universally believe in extended families, so the 'Shen Clan' includes all the siblings, the children, and the grandchildren. For weddings it is expected that *everyone* will attend. For funerals it is expected that *everyone* will attend, and ideally wear the appropriate color for your generation. It doesn't matter where you live, or what you are currently doing, you are expected.

For smaller occasions, we might have a part of the clan. Recently we had a part of the clan that included a seventeen-year-old girl. I will call her 'S'. S was just starting to think about which colleges to apply to next year. Her great interests were art and Japanese culture. S was also interested in combining them together to produce anime, manga, and maybe even gaming art. As you will read elsewhere, I have a little bit of experience with these things. And I am strongly connected to incredibly artistic people: artists who are among the best on the planet.

One artist I knew was an exceptional concept artist, and she had directed me to an amazingly beautiful game called Heavenly Sword. So I mention my background to S, and mention the game too as a reference point. Young people today actually use game references as a communication mechanism. If you do not know the games, it will sound like Tamarian to you. And if you don't know Star Trek, you need to spend a few days and catch up on a few episodes. I'll wait here.

So I have this perfect person who could help S learn to be a great artist. And if she didn't work out, I have many other people who could help S. And I offer to make these connections happen for S. All she does is have to send me her email. I had to run off to oversee my robotics club, but I tell her "just send me your email". I also tell

her mother, who is my cousin and older than me by a bit, "just send me your daughter's email". I have been a part of the Shen Clan for 30 years. For longer than S has been alive. I am an elder in the family, offering to help out another family member. It was a no brainer.

It is now two months later. I have not received any email. S has not benefitted from the talent I could make available to her. S and her mother have blocked chakras. It makes me very sad.

Programming: Math

Tens are a lie. Or at least they are quite rare. You confidently hand someone a ten-dollar-bill for an eight-dollar meal, and it is only by convention that they don't stare at you blankly, expecting you to hand them three more. "Heresy", "Lunacy", "You are completely insane". Yes, I know you are thinking all these things and more, but I assure you I am sane. This particular red pill I took many, many years ago, and all of us who have taken it see the world differently from those that have not. We see numbers correctly, and can understand interesting, useful, and even powerful number systems. Number systems that turn that ten dollar bill into either $2 or even $32. Let us start at $2.

Just as tens are a lie in your daily life, "twos" would be a lie in what is called binary, or base-two, mathematics. In base-two there are no twos. Just "0" (zero) and "1" (one). The digit "2" (two) is not invited to the party. With just the digits "0" and "1", you can represent any number[31] that you need. Say you needed to pay an eight-dollar tab. You would pay that with what might look like an *thousand* dollar bill. $1000 (base-2). Wow! Wouldn't that make someone's day!

Alas, those nice '0's strung in a row do not represent what the server was hoping. For each zero represents multiplying by *two*, not by *ten*. The "multiplying by" is where the "base" comes in. Base-two has no visible twos, but it has a lot of implicit twos. '10' (looks

[31] With certain caveats that I will not bore you with

like a ten right?) is actually "two". Take the '1' and multiply it by '2' for as many digits are to the right of it. Only one digit is to the right (the '0'), so it is worth "two". That thousand-dollar bill has three digits to the right of the '1', so that '1' is actually worth an 8 (2x2x2), and with that you paid the bill off exactly.

Three • point three

The Evant project continued through the summer, and product development was going incredibly well. I was responsible for everything inside the planning system and we had tests and performance metrics showing how well and how fast this "engine" ran. By doing some unconventional things under the covers, the engine was incredibly fast, flexible, and scalable.

At the same time, our product was relatively powerful and intuitive to use from the outside. Part of this was due to 'E' the GUI programmer. 'E' was young but quite talented and well-focused. He built a very pleasant-to-use UI on top of my engine in a then-new language called JavaScript. Very nice UI that worked in any reasonable web browser. This has now become the norm, but Evant was twelve years ago, so this was definitely leading edge then.

Day after day 'E' and I and a few others would make good progress. Finally, by late in the Summer we had made such good progress that Staples said "Yes!" and the company had a signed contract in its pocket.

Then something happened. I know the founders of Evant quite well (one of them attended our wedding), so I could simply ask "Why?" After a few startups, you can guess the reasons for things and certain topics can be hard to discuss for the founders, so I have never asked the question.

At the end of the summer, Rebecca, Maya, and I went to Europe for a wedding in Switzerland. By the time we returned, Evant was gone.

Fini Three

Startups: Stock

In a startup there are two major classes of stocks: Common and Preferred. Common is what founders and employees get. And Preferred is what anyone who puts real money into the startup gets. The main point of Preferred Stock is that if things go south, Preferred gets its money back. The money put in by the preferred shareholders doesn't get spread out to all the sweat-equity[32] common holders "any time soon" or "any time things go awry". Real money in actually never goes to commoners, unless the real money is really happy.

The prefix "Preferred" actually implies much more. Preferred Stock can get any number of preferences. They could get triple their money back. They could have a very unusual conversion to Common. They basically could have almost anything you could write in English. But in a well-run startup, Preferred has protection in case of failure, and a conversion ratio (usually a bit less than 1-1, e.g. 1 to 0.9) to Common if things go well. Common wants Preferred to convert, because until Preferred converts, Common gets nothing. After they convert, everyone is happy… depending on dilution.

Love: Car

Not having a car in Los Angeles is like being stuck in jail. Yes, the jailor will make sure you have food and water, and you have plenty of hours in the day, but you can't really enjoy those hours (your life) at all. Pasadena is a pleasant town, but on foot or on bike, most of it is fairly inaccessible to the kind of students who can get into Caltech. Caltech students would walk a couple city blocks, get to Lake Avenue, and eat whatever was available there. I did this maybe once or twice. The food was not very good. And the whole universe of Los Angeles was hundred if not thousands of city blocks. It was beyond the horizon of carless Caltech students.

---

32 Sweat-equity is ownership of the company based on your labor. Over time, you sweat-equity can increase to very large proportions, but the reality of startups is that your sweat can beat real money put into the company… pretty much never

I grew up outside Philadelphia, and my senior year of high school required me to shuffle between home, Shipley School, and Bryn Mawr College. I am sure I could have somehow done that by busses and mass transit, but my parents graciously gave me a car to help with the commuting: a Diesel Rabbit. I *loved* driving. The Rabbit was front-wheel drive and in the winter the back end could break free on the snow. It was a rush.

When I was accepted to Caltech, it was obvious how I would get there. I was going to drive. I had a car, and it was coming with me. My car was upgraded from a used Rabbit to a used Celica because we were not sure the Rabbit was up to the three thousand mile trip. So as a freshman in Caltech, after having viewed the Grand Canyon, I had a car. There were surprisingly few of us, and even fewer amongst the freshman.

So while boys glommed young women, a certain group of people glommed the drivers. Broadly speaking, those people either loved cars or they loved food. Rebecca loves food.

Right: People

Evant had done a pretty good job of getting the right people to be working on the "last, best, hope". Evant had grown dramatically in its hay day, but 9-11 and other aspects caused me to see a very distilled version of the company. But it seemed as though the distilled version had all the necessary ingredients for (a) understanding customers, (b) defining a solution to their problems, (c) building the solution, and (d) delivering that solution to the customer. That is not very easy to cover when your company shrinks. Usually somebody important leaves and is hard to replace. But Evant had managed to keep most of what it needed and then by adding me, we had the complete package.

One of the problem with any smaller company is that people commonly want to have people *like them* around. So an extroverted CEO wants some similar people to hang with. Or the main engineer wants another person who understands them, their lingo, and their motivations. For a startup, this is quite counter-productive. You

need to get the most done with the fewest people, so any time you see two similar people, you are seeing waste. Yes, people have to understand each other. But that is building a bridge between different skill, not increasing the head count of a particular skill.

All of the most successful startups I have been apart of, had a lot of diversity (skill coverage) near the CEO and only had repetition where some task takes too many hours a week to do. Too many is based on "beyond sixty" or even "beyond eighty" in Silicon Valley, but it could be a lower number as long as the team is being very productive with its time.

Wrong: Stealth

Part of the reason Evant had a challenge before it is that Evant wanted to be "stealthy". The founders of Evant knew me, long before they founded Evant. They knew what I could do, and that I was the *perfect* technical lead for the company. Three years earlier I could have easily been a part of the founding team. Except for "stealth".

When beginning entrepreneurs have a great idea (or so they think), they don't want anyone else to know about it. It is a secret! The idea is so amazing that if someone else found out about it, they would run with the idea and all would be lost! Billions of dollars gone from the poor entrepreneur because someone stole their idea. Very sad when it happens.

Except it basically *never* happens. You either have such a bizarre idea (e.g. "We are going to read through and index *every page* of the internet and let people search all over it") that no one understands it until it happens (Google). Or you have such an incredibly obvious idea (e.g. "We are going to provide free videos") that everyone understand it and says "That is a nice idea, has been done before, and will never make any money" (YouTube). Or some interesting combination of the two. Not sure what people in general think of "FaceLick.com" since I don't pitch it to the usual backers of VCs[33]

[33] Venture Capitalists:

and cofounders.

In spite of it never happening, entrepreneurs and cofounders are all incredibly worried about it. So they try to make employees and funders sign Non-Disclosure Agreements (NDAs) and avoid anyone knowing what they are doing until the time is right. And then the time is right and they have to now drum up interest in their secret organization. All the while, they are burning through the investments made in the company.

And with this summary, you may be able to see the problems. To get valuable people interested in your company and product, *they must know it exists*! But if you were a stealthy founder, you are spending your time hiding and burning through all that time and money. And all the people that could have found out about you and helped you during that stealth period have gone away (people are busy). So effectively you are simply flushing away time and money while being in stealth mode. All the great ideas that *you don't yet know* are lost! You still only have that one great idea you started with.

Like hiding in a cave with something too precious to reveal.

Kindness: Bunnies

My family vacationed in Cape Cod, Massachusetts. Philadelphia in August is very much like a green house with all the controls turned way too high. So we escaped the green house by going a bit north and a bit closer to the ocean. Some years we rented a house on Scraggy Neck, which had direct access to a bay and a friendly dog that loved to chase balls thrown into that bay. This was very nice, but was somewhat isolating (except for the dog). Other years we went to a resort on Chatham Bars. The resort was wonderful: I could go where I wanted, and the staff of the resort was amazingly friendly. I would guess I was about eight years old. And this may have been my first experience of the true definition of "family": we are all family… if we want to be.

Yes, I was a privileged guest who didn't need to do any chores. But it felt more like I was a child in this wonderful extended family

who was given a lot of slack because it was summer. So I would see my new sister, Priscilla, at breakfast, and she was nice enough to serve me a great meal. I would see a new brother in the middle of the day who would teach me how to sail. And I would see him again at night when he would be helping out with dinner. I have a horrible time remembering people's names, and now compensate for my handicaps by putting people's names into my iPhone and repeating them to myself a couple times. I only recently developed this habit and skill. But when writing this section "Priscilla" just came to me. She was part of my family, so of course I can remember her name.

We went to Chatham Bars multiple times, so that also made it seem like the resort was my extended home. I would wander all over the resort grounds: I might go fishing in the morning or swimming in the afternoon. The resort had well-defined boundaries and was reasonably secluded, so my parents were sure of my safety and let me roam as I wished.

One morning, when maybe going out to fish, I encountered a bunny. The bunny had not had a good day. Apparently it argued with a cat or other predator, and although it (or maybe I) convinced that other animal to go away, the other animal had done some serious damage in the process. A rear leg was not really attached anymore, and blood was coming from many different parts of the bunny. But the bunny was alive. It was incredibly cute.

I picked up the bunny, and held it. I had never had something so small, cute, and cuddly in my hands before. I so wanted to keep this incredible source of happiness as my pet. Too have my own little bunny, which I would take care of and it would make me happy.

But the extent of the injuries made it obvious that this was not to be. I had an incredibly cute little bunny that was experiencing incredible pain, and would be dead eventually. At about eight or maybe ten years of age, I did my what I believe was my first, and I know was amongst my hardest, acts of kindness. I drowned a baby bunny.

FOUR

Evant exited by being acquired by Nonstop Solutions. The acquisition occurred when I was in Venice on a trip. I know it occurred then because I got a call while Rebecca, Maya, and I were there: “Hey Mark, we need you to sign some paperwork”. The paperwork was to give me Series-A shares in this acquiring company in exchange for some cash (actually, a lot of cash) Evant owed me. At the time, I would have preferred the cash. But as of today, I enjoyed having these Series-A shares and what their ownership revealed to me about startup investors.

Nonstop was not very far from Evant, so the story is that people wheeled their chairs by Union Square to the new location. All this happened while I was in Europe, so I just have to believe the stories.

Somehow I naturally floated into Nonstop as a consultant. Basically the product wasn’t truly done, it was just complete enough that someone was willing to pay for it. And Nonstop was big enough that they could pay my normal consulting rate, so there was no barrier for me. I simply drove in to a different parking lot, and sat in a different chair.

This continuation of the status quo lasted until about January. Possibly during the closing of the financial records, or the ‘letting go’ of a temporary consulting team unrelated to me, or some other financial audit, I ‘popped’. I get paid far less than I am worth, but significantly more than most people. And if you pay me for several months vs. a few days, the number does grow linearly.

So I get called in by the head of engineering to discuss converting to being a well-paid an employee. I would be paid quite a bit less, but I could work more hours and have more responsibilities. That isn’t really a very good offer. And they can’t really let me go or very bad things would likely happen.

Strangely though, even when I hold all the cards, I am a pretty nice negotiator. Fairly quickly we managed to work out something

that made reasonable sense. Katrina was just a couple months old. We recently moved into our first rental house in Palo Alto. So my expense profile was relatively well defined. And having more of an impact on companies is something I enjoy.

So with some financial changes and a couple perks thrown into the offer, I was on my way to becoming the Director of APT (Architecture, Process, and Technology) for all of Evant, reporting to the VP of Engineering.

Family: Western, Eastern, Atomic

I have three families. My core family is based out of Rebecca and me. It includes Rebecca, Maya, and Katrina. Together we are "home". My atomic family is larger than a standard 'Western' definition. It includes anyone who needs our help and is willing to join in our mission. I commonly make offers to others to join my atomic family, which are meant to be permanent offers, but usually people only take them up transitorily. My nephew 'A' is part of my atomic family. At any time, he can fly, hitchhike, or somehow migrate from Seattle to Palo Alto and he will simply be part of our home. He is allowed to leave at any time, but if he didn't, I would be very happy. My eldest sister could do the same from Cornell. My parents from Philadelphia. Various Ohlone[34], GMS, and PaloBots parents could simply leave their children or themselves at our door, and my atomic family would grow to include them. I believe atoms can be of any size.

I have two kinds of extended families, which are based off Rebecca and my grandparents. That is, my "Eastern" extended family is based off Rebecca's four grandparents, and my "Western" extended family is based off my four grandparents. Amusingly, my Western family lives mostly three thousand miles east of me, and my Eastern family lives mostly to the west of me. Apparently early mapmakers and explorers did not consider America very important.

---

[34] Ohlone elementary is a special school in Palo Alto which educated both of our daughters. GMS is The Girls Middle School, also in Palo Alto currently. And PaloBots is a robotics club for kids that I have run for many years.

Stock: Dilution

The two great banes of an employees in a startup are: (a) the startup failing, in which case they get nothing, or (b) the startup taking in so much money that whatever percentage the employees originally owned, on exit those employees have very little. Say I owned 10% of a company Foo[35] before Foo has received any external validation of its value. That external validation is almost always the Series-A investors: the first 'preferred' investors who are putting their money into the company expecting to get more money out. The company is valued *before* this external money is put into it, and then the two values (abstract and tangible) are combined. If I owned 10% of Foo, and Foo needs $5MM[36] dollars to really make it to the next round, my ownership "post-money" is completely dependent on the valuation of Foo "pre-money". If Foo is deemed to be far enough along as a business that it is worth $5MM by itself, than I own $500K on paper. After the external money, I will own 5% of a $10MM company that has a fresh new $5MM in cash in the bank. I will have been diluted in percentage by half, but I will still own $500K on paper. That would be a very good dilution.

On the other hand, if Foo is deemed to be worth only $1MM, then I own $100K on paper and after the $5MM, I will own less than 2% of the company. That would be unpleasant given how much time and effort I put into the startup over the years I worked their.

But these numbers show the only sane way to figure out what financial and other sacrifices you should make for the startup equity. Never think of 'what could it be worth?' if it succeeds. That is making *you* take all the risk, and startups are a very risky business. Instead think 'what is it worth now?' Getting something worth $100K over four years is getting a $25K bonus. Getting $500K over four years is five times better. But it is still not a windfall. The people that get the windfalls are *lucky*, nothing more. Get what you are worth and the luck goes away. You could be very unlucky like

---

[35] Foo is a common way to name something in pseudo-programming. It is followed by "Bar" and "Baz". In actual programming, you should use more meaningful names, but "Foo" is quite fun.

[36] MM is a symbol for million, K is a symbol for thousand.

me, and still be very successful and happy. Well, actually, happiness is totally "orthogonal"[37].

Four • point two

Surprisingly, Evant let the current VP of Engineering go just after I was hired. This was unfortunate: I did not know him very well (he worked out of Atlanta), but he had seemed a reasonable person in our interactions. The VP of Engineering is a fairly important role in a large product company. The VPE leads the people who transform the vision of the CEO and Product Design teams into the actual products that the company sells. Leading software developers is similar to herding cats. And by cat I mean to span the range of personalities from kittens through Maine Coons and onward to Lions and Tigers. Lots of different kinds of cats, which need to work effectively together.

So Evant needed a VP of Engineering. Evant was apparently very lazy about finding a reasonable replacement. They looked in the office next to the departed, and found an older man. That was apparently all the screening process required. I will call him 'T'.

T was experienced, but not in any way that would help Evant run a team of actual people. When I "lead" people, I try to put myself (and my cubicle) in the center of everything. You can't lead people you don't know. And you can't lead people from behind a door. You can't really lead people at all: you can show them where you want them to go, and then prove to them, by words and action, that where you want to go is where they want to go too. We all want to go *there*. Let's do it together.

T hid in Atlanta, the smallest office Evant had. Even worse, he hid in his office in Atlanta. That was the biggest office in the smallest office, and it also had a closeable door. And apparently it was normally closed. At least that is what friends and coworkers in

---

[37] Orthogonal is a very nerdy but very powerful word. It means "on a different dimension" and "in no way connected to the other dimensions". Forward and backwards are orthogonal to leftward and rightward. North and South are orthogonal to East and West.

Atlanta told me. T was "leading" from behind closed doors. That doesn't work.

Over time, it was clear that T was never going to transform and actually do the job of dealing with the Evant development team. Evant engineering had to do a company-wide salary review, and T knew nothing about anyone. We had product delivery issues in Atlanta and San Francisco, and T could not help any of the teams on the ground. I saw T fly into San Francisco for executive management meetings, but I do not know if the executive team valued his input, and nothing valuable ever came out to the team from these flights. And then T started giving very strange, very negative, and very unproductive feedback to people in San Francisco. He started punishing hard-working team members. Not doing anything useful is one thing, but hurting team members was quite another.

I immediately started escalating the issues associated with T to the COO[38] and CEO[39]. I believe they told T to lay off, and eventually changed his title to something different from VP of Engineering. Because I cared to do what was right and necessary for the engineering team, I was now Evant's VP of Engineering. I was VPE in action, that's due to a lack of anyone else having the title, and with the slightest of support of the C-level of the company. I was *acting* VP of Engineering.

Failure: Grades

I mentioned I had no problem with grades at Caltech. That is because I never cared much at all about grades at Caltech. Somehow I realized during my freshman year that to just *survive* Caltech I had to change to a new grading system. And so I came up with this one: An 'F' is an 'F', anything higher is a 'P' (for pass), except an 'A' is an 'A'. That might sound peculiar or even insane, but only by that insanity could I have possibly graduated from Caltech. Further, to

---

[38] Chief Operating Officer: the person that runs day-to-day operations of a company

[39] Chief Executive Officer: the person accountable to the Board of Directors for *everything* about the company.

disprove my supposed insanity, I have indirect empirical data that this was the *correct* grading system. Using any other grading system (but one) at Caltech was insane.

As we approached graduation, say Junior year, we started attending various meetings sponsored by the Caltech Gnome Club. The Gnome Club is Caltech's alumni club, and the meetings were post-graduation oriented. Basically, they were about getting jobs for those who were not going down the academic doctorate path.

The Gnomes had surveyed Caltech alumni over the years to figure out how well they were doing. I believe they thought they had pretty good data, and being Caltech alumni, they new the standards they were supposed to always *exceed*, so I will trust them in their observations. These Gnomes noticed one very interesting thing about Caltech graduates. Unlike what people might expect, and maybe unlike the case at other universities, there was *absolutely no* statistical correlation between final GPA and pretty much anything. Life earnings… Nope. Happiness… Nope.

There was only one variable that affected those things. Graduating. Those who didn't graduate, who flamed out[40], earned less. So you just had to graduate to get your reward. Every class you pass gets you closer to graduating. Each 'P' in freshman year, and each 'Not F' every year thereafter. The only other correct grade system is to drop my "an 'A' is an 'A'". That would be the simplest correct grade system. I kept the 'A's because I was proud of the 'A's. They were almost always in classes I loved, or because I really worked my ass off. So they may not have helped my life earnings, but they did help my happiness. They reinforced my passions.

Four • point three

The first thing, the most important thing, an *acting* VP of Engineering should do, is find a replacement. I had no desire to be in the role. I chose to join Evant to be *under* someone that was a good VP of

[40] Flamed out: did not graduate, but ideally with some kind of final flare for the dramatic like dancing around naked in Milliken pond

Engineering (or so I thought). I became *acting* VP of Engineering due to a vacuum and a team with many needs. But I am a hands-on kind of guy, and dealing with middle-managers who wanted my job, and "peers" who thought I didn't belong at the executive table, were not things that interested me. But I greatly cared about the team, so I wanted to get a good person to replace me. All of the executive team were aligned with me on this one topic alone: get rid of me and get someone better.

I must have interviewed more than a dozen people over much less than a half-dozen months. I said "yes" to greater than half of them. But every time, someone else said no. Evant was in a great stage for a startup. We had a lot of money coming in from major customers, and there was still many ways to give out significant equity in the startup. The team was large enough that a management-oriented VP made sense. Getting good VPEs to be interested was not hard. But one after one, I would say yes, and someone else would say no.

This rhythm went on month after month even into the next year. At some point, the CEO simply stopped looking. No more candidates came into the pipeline. Either I was doing a good-enough job, or he was simply tired of the strain the hiring process put on the team.

Or maybe both.

Math • point two

With the core of math bases defined, I will now show you *my favorite* base, and one of the few that truly does have tens in it. It is base-32: it has a total of 32 digits in it! And one of those digits is a ten. Simply labeled 'a'. Revealing the whole system is pretty quick, and likely very familiar: "0123456789abcdefghjkmnpqrs tvwxyz". In this, an 'a' is worth 10 (decimal) and the 'z' is worth 31 (decimal). As with all other systems, the name of the system (base-32) is always the digit that is missing.

Base-32 is *awesome.* By having these extra digits you can represent

very large numbers very quickly. Say you need to buy a $15,000 (decimal) car, in base 32, that would just be "$emr". Saved half the space if you include the comma! Another fun trick with base 32 is you can easily create version stamps, and with them have a quick way to create "vector clocks"[41]. But that story is reserved for a different book.

Four • point four

In the winter and spring, the Evant executive team had a number of meetings discussing augmenting our San Francisco and Atlanta development teams with an India-based team. I had run through various analyses of creating an India office, estimating engineering costs realistically based on guessed productivity of the India team that companies like IBM were suggesting. We had a lot of different analyses, none of which showed some amazing bump in development output per dollar but many of which showed improving the development expense numbers. If we could get a descent team in India, we could maybe double one or two product line's output for much less than doing it locally.

For several months, we talked sporadically about launching an offshore team. Each conversation would have more information, but no more resolution than the one before. Then in April, something changed. The CEO must have talked with someone, or some financial model changed, or Evant was preparing to sell itself (unbeknownst to me) and instead of a closing "we need to discuss this some more next time", the meeting ends with "we are doing this, now".

Homes: Mobile

Mobile homes are very misnamed. Yes, they are mobile before you settle into them. You can see them moving down highways, especially in Lancaster, Pennsylvania. But before you move into your mobile home, you must 'plant' it into the ground, and from that

---

[41] vector clock: A way to track what version a group of entities is at for a given piece of information

point forward it will never move again. This can be extremely unfortunate for the residents, because if someone else owns the land, and that land is located in Palo Alto, then someone else will eventually (inevitably) sell that land. Land that is worth more than all the residents will ever make in their lives… combined.

Four • point five

By the time of the India offshore project for Evant (I called it "Bang!"), I am professionally transforming from an engineer into an execution specialist: someone who makes things happen. This may seem like an impossible title. How can you just make things happen? Aren't there things you can not make happen? Things you shouldn't make happen? Those are good questions, but irrelevant to an execution specialist. An execution specialist will try to make *anything* happen within their moral boundaries. It is acceptable to fail. It is a failure to not try.

When I finally received the "We are doing this" for the India office, I was neither happy or sad. Instead, I was energized, alert, and incredibly active. I now had to solve a lot of problems. I had a newborn daughter, a toddler, and a wife I adore. Would they come to India with me? If not, would I go without them? Luckily Rebecca loves me enough to not make me chose, and my whole family was ready to venture twelve time zones away for several months.

India is a place, but we are going there for the people not the location. Who would these people be? How do I recruit and select a team thousands of miles away? How good a team could I get? How would I train them? What equipment would we have? How would I train the team in the US to work with the team there? The questions just kept coming and coming. But again, this is not daunting to an execution specialist. You simply do your best to write down and answer each question. Right now. To the best of your ability. You can change your answer later if need be or if new knowledge presents itself. But you can't *delay* answering the question. That is not trying.

After a brief visit to Taiwan, my family and a coworker 'C' landed

in the Bangalore airport late at night with suitcases full of computers. We took a limo to our hotel: the Leela of Bangalore. The Leela would be our base as we looked for proper housing for an extended stay, and later became our refuge from the grit of the "Garden City".

It was a mere eight weeks from when the go ahead was given.

Love: Women

Females are clearly the superior gender. Put one hundred women and two men on a deserted island, and they will have a great chance of building a thriving new community. Switch those numbers, and they will be lucky to survive the week. So females are innately superior and the ratio should really be maybe 10:1 in their favor. Strangely, nature doesn't seem to agree and makes the odds one to one. And mothers, seeing the misshapen baby boys in front of them, take pity on them and raise them like their own. Mothers are wonderful.

Whether or not men remember this blessing from women in their home lives, they definitely don't seem to remember it in their working worlds. Women are treated very badly by men. Some men may be intentionally treating women differently, and those men are "words I will not use in print". But I think the more insidious problem is that many men behave badly to *everyone* and it is just that women are currently more susceptible to the bad behavior.

Women would have thrived in my *very classy* startup number two (DSG). I think the many female employees who were in startup three (small Evant) were treated very well, but you would have to check with them to be sure. One additional startup after those two might have been good to women. So excluding my own startup due to possible bias, I would say that only three of the nine startups I have been a part of had an environment that was respectful of women. That the spirit from the CEO downward would make sure women were treated well and equally. That is 33%.

In the rest of the startups, I am minimally aware of some actual gender bigotry. But I am totally aware of female-punishing

activities. One startup in particular had a CEO that was so strong willed, eloquent, handsome, and even 'cute' that it was hard for women to resist him. Unfortunately for them, he was an optimizer, and wanted to optimize their salary, their free time, and their freedom away from them. My interactions with him were fine. I received significant promotions, raises, and independence. Within a few months, I could do whatever I wanted to do because of two things (a) I was visibly and dramatically helping him make his startup succeed, and (b) I made it completely clear through my words and actions that I would do what I wanted. What I wanted to do were all the right things to make the company successful and the team happy. But it also included walking out the door if anyone stopped me from doing what I wanted. The CEO did not like the second rule, but he liked me. A lot. And respected me. Also a lot. He wrote my headline reference on LinkedIn.

Unfortunately for them, that company had two women, and both of them were treated very badly. One was paid poorly and forced to either never leave the office or to be on-call any moment she did. Another was paid poorly and could never change her state even when she should have an amazing upper hand. Even when she had the power to walk out the door. Walk out the door to a better life.

Four • point six

Bangalore has slums. And one of them is located right outside the Leela. It was very difficult emotionally to leave our refuge and immediately witness abject poverty. We ultimately had an air-conditioned car, with a fantastic driver 'R' who took very good care of my family the whole time we were in India. And we had plenty of Rupees to pay for good food. So we were fairly protected from anything other than illness. But we did not close our eyes to what we saw around us. And some of the richest of the poor were carrying broken stones around on their heads. I don't know what that employment paid, but it is hard to conceive it amounted to more than just table scraps to keep them alive another day. How do you explain that to a three year old girl? To make her feel lucky but not guilty?

India has a lot of really nice people. Maybe among the most jovial people I have ever hung out with. If they are making a good living, they are generally amazingly happy. At the end of any given working day or week, they do what they think would be fun: maybe bowling, maybe traveling, maybe working out in a gym for hours on end, and definitely eating. Many Indians are very religious, but it is an observance of religion that is incredibly tolerant: "I worship Vishnu, you worship something else. Just don't offend my household and everything is awesome."

India is also incredibly diverse. Back in 2003, there were relatively few India states that had expatriates present in the US. But within Bangalore, people from every state are present. This gives a diversity of names (e.g. "Rex") and a diversity of culture. Getting all these diverse people to get along was not a difficult process because of the tolerance and happiness. But getting tolerant and happy people to be productive is actually a very big challenge. And although I could enjoy my time in India, I was there to make something very concrete happen: to have a productive and less expensive development center for Evant.

One week in, and I did not have that yet. But the process was starting.

Love: India

Living in a country like India teaches you about yourself as much as it teaches you about other people. Each of us has many assumptions built into us based on where we grew up and how our family behaves. These assumptions become our "norm" and as an adult you somehow decide that all the world should be normal relative to us. But the world isn't "normal". There is no normal behavior that spans the entire planet earth. And when you move twelve time zones away, and move into the actual homes of the people twelve time zones away, and you keep your eyes and mind open, you learn.

First you learn that bovines can be a common part of your every day living. You take a walk around the neighborhood and the neighborhood cow is taking a walk around too. You drive down a

street and must stop at an intersection because a cart pulled by water buffalo is traveling out of control and would broadside you if you ventured forward a little bit further. In the US, cows are not nearly this common: they hang out in fields you drive buy on the interstate or on farms that most Americans do not even see. All American bovines seem to be relative content and controlled with their lot in life, so the day cows take to the streets of American cities is probably far in the future.

Water in India is not innately drinkable. This too is a bizarre situation to someone from a highly developed country. In theory you can drink toilet water in America or Taiwan. I wouldn't recommend it, and I have not done it myself. But I do believe I would survive the experience as long as I flushed a few times first. Drinking the water from a no-click bottle in India could possibly be fatal. At least 'C' protected me from that once, and I trust that 'C' knows India quite well.

A no-click bottle is bottle water from a labeled bottle water container, so it should be thoroughly safe. But when they twisted the top, there were no clicks. The seal was not clearly broken when they served the bottled water to you. Please do not drink this water. You don't know what is in there, and the establishment that served it has enough time and energy on its hands to *refill* plastic containers. Whether their food is any good, you can decide. But don't drink their water until it clearly 'clicks'. Or change to beer.

Four • point seven

Continuing with my water obsession, if you live in the common populated parts of the US, water works like this: fully drinkable (potable) water comes from the street with quite a bit of water pressure to let you do lots of things with it. There is a meter that measures how much pressurized and drinkable water you get from the city or county, but there is no meter for how much waste water you gave back. Trash in the US is either free or simply expected and part of your baseline monthly bills.

Within a US home, some of the potable water is given out to the

plants surrounding the house. No, American plants are not some alien breed that needs human-drinkable water. They might not even like human-potable water. But our watering systems automatically spray this unadulterated water on the highly adulterated grasses that create our luscious lawns before that water had a chance to go anywhere else.

Alternatively, the drinkable water is sent into our toilets. Yes, you can drink from the toilets. Not sure why you would want to, but if you ask American dogs and cats, they will tell you the water is quite healthy to drink. Many cats live long and prospurr on it.

Yet another alternative: some of the water is sent into a modest-sized holding tank where it gets heated to a nice toasty temperature. This is so you can waste long parts of your day with warm water showering down on you. Kind of like simulating you are living in some tropical paradise or maybe even India.

Except in India this is not how water works at all. At least it wasn't how it worked when we were there.

Drinkable water in India comes in bottles. Small Coke bottles in restaurants. Large multi-gallon Coke bottles in your home. All the bottles have clickers. Don't drink from bottles that don't click when you open them. You don't know what is in them. Coke guarantees water is in water bottles and Coke is in Coke bottles. Guarantees in India are quite rare, so take advantage of them when you can.

The rest of the water in India is both initially cold and forever non-potable. That sounds like a drawback, but it is actually just a difference and has both benefits and issues. But because it is such a large difference, a lot of US assumptions about water are completely wrong when you are in India.

In the house we rented in India, water could come from the street. Could, but didn't have to. Turn the water off from the street in India, and your house goes "off the grid". Then a truck can bring the water periodically, depending on your storage capacity and consumption. We had a huge cistern beneath our house that had

many days worth of water, so maybe a truck had to visit us once a week. In contrast, turn off the water from the street to a house in the United States, and your house is dead in the (lack of) water. Open minded "Survivalists" in the US could learn a great deal from living in India for a couple months.

Employment: Salary

Americans of European decent generally don't like talking about salaries. Growing up, I never really knew what my parents made. And when starting out in the workforce, it seemed like it was taboo to discuss it. I believe some companies have written policies against discussing salary. And after I found out a coworker's salary, my first startup fired me on the spot. There is a lot of evidence that American companies do not want people to trade salary information.

American companies want a lot of things. And many of these things are *completely illegal,* especially in California. Companies want you to sign non-competes. Generally illegal. Not paying you for unused vacation. Completely illegal. The list goes on and on. I had one startup simply stop paying me my full wages. It turns out California has a simple three-page form to correct and punish that illegal behavior. But in most cases, a company can get by with it because (a) employees don't know the law and (b) employees have seen the practice before so they think it is normal and legal.

Presumably some companies don't want people knowing other employees' wages so they can't bargain for raises effectively. Maybe some people are getting paid ridiculous salaries: either ridiculously high or ridiculously low. Or the salaries would appear to be arbitrary numbers.

While acting as VPE[42] for Evant, I rebalanced the salaries of all the engineers and technical managers. I had a very simple model, basically equivalent to tennis-playing Levels. In tennis you have formal level definitions within the USTA. For example:

---

[42] Vice-President of Engineering

> **4.5** You have developed your use of power and spin and can handle pace. You have sound footwork, can control depth of shots, and attempt to vary game plan according to your opponents. You can hit first serves with power and accuracy and place the second serve. You tend to over hit on difficult shots. Aggressive net play is common in doubles.[43]

With such a definition, any player can very easily get a general feel of their level. Then he or she can go out and play people who either similarly 'guessed' their levels or who did a more rigorous level test. If the first player consistently plays better than the others, he or she is are at least their level. If not, he or she may be a level or so lower.

I considered this a very fair idea, so did it with the whole team. You can't go mano-a-mano in software very easily, but peers and managers can easily figure out what general level someone is compared to his or her various peers. And it is also not very painful: it doesn't feel like they are are insulting anyone; they are just comparing people to each other and saying "I think these two people provide about the same contribution to the company; that this third person provides more; …" and so on.

So with a team of select peers, team managers, and me… we leveled everyone. I hoped to have a fair amount of agreement, but given that I knew people pretty well (including the levelers), I was sure I could fairly determine "inconclusive" employees.

Next I leveraged a human-resources tool called the Radford Survey. This surveyed companies to figure out what these companies paid different positions and different skill levels within a particular position. To make it so the different companies gave salaries for approximately similar kinds of work, they formally defined all the kinds of jobs out there, and they defined six levels of skill within a job.

The Radford levels read similarly to the tennis levels. For

43 USTA NTRP Level 4.5

example:

> *Level 3:*
>
> **KNOWLEDGE:** Uses skills as a seasoned, experienced professional with a full understanding of industry practices and company policies and procedures; resolves a wide range of issues in imaginative as well as practical ways. This job is the fully qualified, career-oriented, journey-level position.
>
> **JOB COMPLEXITY:** Works on problems of diverse scope where analysis of data requires evaluation of identifiable factors. Demonstrates good judgment in selecting methods and techniques for obtaining solutions. Interacts with senior internal and external personnel.
>
> **SUPERVISION:** Normally receives little instruction on day-to-day work, general instructions on new assignments.[44]

The Radford levels provided a basic skeleton of structure, but I needed many more gradations. Almost all employees were either threes or fours, and using just two levels would have made the whole thing useless. So I augmented the system and broke each level into four variations, making us have a working eight-sublevels. Finally, I took the different groups of employees and figured out who was clearly a 3.0 (maybe just barely) and who was clearly a 4.0 (again, just barely) and *voila* you have a twenty-four-level system that almost everyone is placed on. Using the Radford salary surveys you can pick how competitive a salary you want to provide. Each sublevel of the twenty-four automatically mapped onto a "competitive" salary. If the CEO changed the competition level, everyone's target salary would automatically adjust.

It took a lot of work, but nothing ridiculous. And although no one outside HR and managers saw the result, if it was revealed nobody *should have been* particularly bothered. We were basically using the tennis model: if someone didn't like their rating and

---

[44] Citation

claimed they were a 4.5 then (a) she had to do everything a 4.5 is expected to do and (b) she had to find who-ever is a 4.5 and show how she was contributing at least that much. It was exposed competition. The competition was always there, exposing it just casts sunlight on it.

The only flaw was when people were paid way *over* their level. We just let that slide, hoping it would be fixed over time.

Four • point nine

While spending several months wrangling with water, I had also managed to wrangle and train a pretty descent development team. Each individual person was not quite "up to snuff" by my fairly lofty software engineering standards, but by pairing or more likely tripling people together, I could manage to get subteams that could get things done as well as (or even better than) their US counterparts. The India team was clearly competent and skilled. On their watch, Evant would make great strides forward for Evant's customers and business strategy. The "Bang!" project was a success. So clearly it is time to party ☺

We had a few major parties near the end of my family's time in India. My favorite by far was a wedding. More specifically 'H's wedding. 'H' was one of the few women on my team and integrating this cool cat in with all the others was not an easy thing. Indian professional work is male-centric, similar to US professional work. We don't seem to have a monopoly on gender bigotry.

And also similar to pre-war US values, Indian women *rule* the home. You enter a home, and you need to figure out which woman runs it. Enter the highest paid executive of Tata's home: find the woman that rules him and say "thank you for letting me be here". He didn't let you in, he just showed you where he lives.

Weddings are traditionally a female affair in a female run home with a lot of females telling lots of males what they should be doing. Augment that event with wrapping all these beautiful females in amazing Saris and it imprints you forever.

Palo Alto: Class

Palo Alto has four or so financial classes. The highest class has so much money that they can easily own their home and do not need to work at all. The money could be "old", or it could be "new". Given the only truly old wealth in California was the land, deer, and flora that was loved by native Americans, any reference to "old money" in California is really "slightly less than new money". Interestingly, by this definition, the many elderly retired people in Palo Alto count as in the highest class. They bought a $50K house and live nicely on their pension. The only issue for them is that purchasing items from Whole Foods seems a bit expensive.

The second class makes *so much* money that they can easily own their home, as long as they keep making *so much* money. When I mention this book to members of this class, some of them say "Yeah right, slums in Palo Alto! Where are they?" These are the cluelessly lucky ones. Others in their class know exactly what I am referring to. They may be making *so much* money today, but Silicon Valley is *brutal* and whole industries simply die or move to Arizona. The second class has a very high level of outsourced parenting. To make sure they make *so much* money, the parents ruthlessly go to work everyday and leave raising their kids to someone else. In one family, the nanny is so amazing and loving that she is clearly the childrens' mother. The parents are like financial servants in the home that the nanny and her daughters live in together.

The third class is the slums. These are families that either rent their home or are knowledgeably near the edge of being able to pay their mortgage. Have a bad month or two, and you are on the street. For my family, the slum-catastrophe-protection-system is primarily based on financial buffers: liquid assets that can pay monthly debts when income is poor. I call them 'Bulkheads'. If I have a dozen bulkheads, then things are in really good shape. As I will describe later, these bulkheads can't deal with all the perils of the slums, but they do handle the main issues.

An interesting part of being in the third class, is that it appears people within it are a bit more "alive". They appreciate their lives

and can have very meaningful conversations with each other about the sacrifices, terrors, and joys that fill their days. In spite of being strapped for money, the third class is the group that *volunteers more* than all the other classes. Raising money for education. Running clubs for kids. Volunteering at schools. Helping kids perform plays. Most of these community-oriented commitments are done by the third class. It is as if the first two classes are really just vacationing in Palo Alto while the rest of us actually live here.

The fourth class is the homeless. I assume most of them are very unhappy and hidden away in some corner under a bridge or within unpleasant special housing. But I know that some of them are actually pretty happy in spite of having no home. 'R' hangs out in a park every day and wanders around a few dozen city blocks. He gets coffee at the same place I get coffee and pays with cash for it. I don't know where the money comes from or where all his travels take him, but I say "Hi!" every time I encounter him in our shared park.

Palo Alto is pretty confused about what to do with the homeless. Periodically laws come through that would force them to move their cars or motor homes into a different city, but these laws got squelched by the US Constitution. I think the biggest issue with the homeless is that they are free-thinking people. So you can want them to do all types of things that would be "better for them", but they get to make the ultimate decision themselves. And their values are different from what we project on them.

Four • point ten

We returned from India just after the start of preschool, so some time in September. While in India, I had invited the new VP of Engineering over multiple times, but for various reasons he never came. It was once even completely planned out and then at the last minute he canceled. So our only interaction had been over the phone, and even that was never about us but just about the India team. I believe he was with Evant for about two months before I returned, and in that time one of my reports had clearly worked a lot on him. I found this out over coffee at Torrefazione.

Again, my position on India was that is was an extension of the San Francisco team. I trained them to know the Planning Engine as well as anyone in San Francisco could. They might have needed to work in pairs or triplets, but they could do the work. And they could figure out the work themselves: no micro-detailing of tasks to be done. Some people view my position as radical. They want an India team just to be QA[45] or very micro-managed in their daily tasks.

During my discussion with the new VPE, it was clear that he was now strongly in the "some people" camp. So I was in a pretty awkward position. I did not want to be an external-facing CTO and I did not like how the India team was going to be treated after my return. I also thought we had a great idea in how we used technology to make development teams more productive, even handling the massive time and space distance of India. So I quit.

Fini Four

Right: Office

Office space politics is rampant in all sizes of companies. Larger companies have time for this waste of energy. Startups do not. Unfortunately, startups have to deal with different styles, comfort, and convention of their employees. Some companies do without offices and have a big open space. Unfortunately this interferes with having private meetings, recruiting interviews, confidential calls, and true quiet areas for focused work. On the other hand, having too many offices tends to isolate people. This is especially pernicious if management "lives" in their office.

My favorite version is to have central areas that are relatively open but if you "duck your head" you get to be a bit more focused, and then communal offices around the central areas that are sufficient for phone calls, small meetings, and potentially taking time out from any excessive noise in the central area. Ideally the open

[45] Quality Assurance: Basically making sure software does what it is supposed to by either manually interacting with it (running it or looking at it), or ideally by creating automated tests that prove it works without human interaction

area can support two people around a computer for "pairing" when useful.

But another variation that seems to work fine is a collection of two to four person offices that allow easy communication and flow between open rooms, but limits the amount of cross-room noise. There should still be private offices and larger meeting areas available, but they can be pretty limited given you can always ask someone to leave for a little bit .

Wrong: Pace

Startups are not a sprint. Yes, time is short but you don't fix that problem by trying to sprint to some end-zone or major achievement out of the gate. There are a lot of problems with the sprint mentality. First, that major achievement may not be worth anything at all to your customer. You guessed wrong, and the team is now winded and dispirited. Second, even if that major marker is worth something, startups don't exit by hitting a single marker. There are a series of markers following that first marker and you are still be in the race. Yes, there are anomaly startups that get acquired after doing either one or even no notable feat. You can also buy lotto tickets and spend much less effort to get that kind of lucky windfall.

Startups are a race where you need more and more team members pulling their weight and working together. I think of it as a peloton, where some of the team members are building and improving the bikes as you go. At first you have no bikes, so you are just running along scouting out the terrain. Then a few people organize a formation (a plan) and everyone gets into a good stride together. And then bikes start popping up. And then bikes designed for the kinds of terrain the team is seeing. And so on as the team improves its abilities based on understanding the customers, their needs, and how the team can make good progress towards them. So a peloton that is slow (on foot) but observant grows into a set of crazy-fast pelotons that have become honed to the startup's needs. This will get you where you need to go faster than over pushing it at the start.

Yes, people can lose their hurry, but that is easier to keep in their heads ("you have twenty four paychecks left") than helping them recover from being burned out.

Kindness: Business

The business world is very competitive and can be very fickle. For the post-war (World War Two) adults, there was a lot of work to do and not a lot of people to get all that work done. Work seemed abundant and if you put your shoulder into the grindstone, you would be rewarded with shiny new cars, summers on the beach, and a nice retirement. These were the promises of many companies when times are going well and competition for employees is fierce. It may appear that these companies are being very kind, but that is an illusion they want you to believe.

My father's pension was raided before he retired, so he retired on relatively little. My wife is trying to get a job, but is old enough now that she is viewed as "too senior". Some of my startups have kept their employees making way below their value to the company, and even below a living wage, while the CEO lives in a mansion. Business is innately cruel because the owner 'owns' and the employees 'work'. If the owner gets sick, the owner still owns. If the employee gets sick, the employee is not working. A contractor may not get paid. An employee may or may not have some amount of paid-time-off. Either way, money is lost (unused PTO has to be paid to the employee at severance).

So kindness in business is actually a rarity. But I believe I have provided it myself, and I know I have benefitted from it. You are kind in business when you care about the whole person you are dealing with. You meet some of their needs beyond what you competitively have to. I pay people what I believe they are worth instead of the minimum wage they would definitely take. DSG gave me a bonus when the company was sold, and long after I could do anything to better their situation. And one employer told me to go away so I could finish Caltech. That company lost a valuable employee, but I am likely a happier person for finishing college first.

Very kind. I am grateful.

FIVE

My participation in the first four startups had been as an employee or a contractor. I may have been part of the launching team or instrumental to the success of the company, but I was clearly not a founder or co-founder. That all changed with Velidom. I was clearly the founder and president of Velidom: I did all the paperwork of incorporation working with a law firm; I set up the equity tables; and I set up the human resources aspects. Velidom was born in December and had its first employees in early January. It was a giddy time.

We started with five employees. All from Evant. It could have been a lot more, and by the death knells it was very clear it should have been a lot less. When I announced my departure from Evant, a lot of people were interested. I believe it was because people liked working on my teams, or they were interested in what I was proposing to do. At one count it seemed like it could be ten or more.

When negotiating with the CEO over getting the IP rights to the tools we had built at Evant, this threat of losing ten people was clearly on the table. Later Velidom would get two more, so it wasn't a delusion on my part. It was a real possibility. But if it happened either Velidom would have died within months, or we would have changed into a service company with maybe some amount of product development. I wanted Velidom to be a pure product company.

We did some services for Evant to both buy the IP and reduce the departure sting. I normally take several months to work myself out of a company, so in that regard I was unhappy about the abrupt departure. This feeling was mitigated by the facts that I had just trained the India team; that I had been in India for several months and the office wasn't really used to me; and finally that Evant chose to 'promote' me without my inclusion at all (I was in India). So my departure was mitigated, but four other people were not, so we let two to three of them be part-time contractors for Evant while we figured out what Velidom was going to do. What was the problem

we were solving? What were we going to build to solve it? Who would want it? What would they pay and how?

Startups: Size

Size seriously matters. A startup has a runway to launch its products based on the amount of investment it can raise before that launch occurs. After the launch (other people using your product and ideally even paying you money for it), a new runway can normally be created because a lot of people like that stage of a company much more. And with additional successes, yet more runways can be created. Eventually the added investments are really 'acceleration capital' or 'expansion capital' verses being runways.

Payroll is the great propellant down the runway. Payroll doesn't help with getting the product to launch (obviously the people do, but paying them does not), and it can chew up runway very quickly. The fully loaded cost of a normal Silicon Valley engineer was about $200K when Velidom was formed. So if there were five of us, that would mean we needed $2MM to have two years of runway for the Payroll alone. Some people can raise that kind of money pretty easily, but I certainly could not (at least easily).

Dealing with the Payroll problem has two obvious solutions: hire fewer people or pay people less. Velidom did some of the later (if an employee wanted more stock, they could trade salary for equity, and I was paid minimum wage), but Velidom should have done much more of the former and launch with two or three people.

Founding a startup is an act of the truly insane. No sane person would ever invest their time and money into something with no track record, with no customers, and likely with nothing more than a glint of a product. That is just crazy. And yet, if you go insane, you can't really help yourself. And everything seems so promising. And everyone so excited. It is epic and tragic from the first team meeting. Having a lot of people join you in this epic party seems awesome… inspiring. Until it becomes tragic some years later when it dawns on you "Two was enough wasn't it?"

Failure: Rinse and Repeat

The VLSI story did not end where I left it. Let us return to school a year later.

Amazingly, I am taking the same course again. *I am forgetful, and don't recall whether I dropped the class the year before or if I am taking it again for the fun of it. The first sounds more likely. This time around I am with my classmates (the year before I was 'young'). Same contest. We have to design a different circuit but it is a similar kind of problem. This time I put in a ridiculous number of hours to create a great solution. I review my design very carefully. We have slightly better tools this year and are able to simulate*[46] *our circuit: tools are improving every year. Before the homework submission deadline I ask the professor for help. Could he do a sanity check on my design? But he says no.*

We all submit our homework, and the professor or TAs review them all. The next class, the professor shows the outline of all the different solutions. Lots of squares and rectangles inside one another with the smallest in the center. This time I know exactly what this diagram shows.

I recognize my outline because it is slightly distinct this year. Like an 'L' maybe.

It is in the center.

It is not bold.

I manage to pass the course this time, or simply decide to end my self-flagellation: I never take any other courses from that professor.

I still love VLSI.

Five • point two

Velidom had a very successful launch. The team knew each other

[46] To simulate a circuit is to run that circuit as if it were actually physically created. So barring a physical defect (which do occur sporadically), if your circuit simulates properly and has reasonable tolerance for physical defects, your actual chip would work properly

well, and enjoyed working with each other. We knew in general what we were trying to build, and also had a starting implementation that we bought from Evant (with our services). I had a few meetings with prospects early on, who seemed interested. And had feedback from IBM Global Services that they were interested in our product. But our vision was very big: we were going beyond what we had built with Evant and making it both more flexible and more capable. We were also making it a true product, where multiple customers could own it (on their servers), or we could host multiple customers on our servers.

Stock: Dissent

About a year after I left Evant, they were successfully sold to Manhattan Associates. The sale was not at a very good price, and by that point there were Series-C and Series-B shares along with the Series-A and Common. Startup stocks have two very simple core rules: "Preferred gets money before Common", and "Last in, First out". You can have various other rules too based on the actual preferences in a preferred stock, but these rarely affect the core rules. The sale price of Evant was so low that Common was wiped out. This is actually "common" if unfortunate. People with common stock did not put any money in, so if it is a down sale[47], there is no reason for them to expect to get money at all. All the preferred shares put money in, and can reasonably expect to get their money back if at all possible.

Unfortunately the sale price was so low that Series-A was going to get nothing too. I believe that is less common, but it clearly possible. The price was such that Series-C was going to get its money back (actually more than that, based on a preference), and Series-B was going to get its money back. But Series-A was going to get nothing.

I was not amused. I had received Series-A stock in lieu of cash owed to me, and I wanted *my money* back. I had been a nice guy to

---

47 A sale valued less than the company was worth during prior valuations for A, B, and C (in reverse order).

let them give me stock at the time, but I am not a pushover. So when I received a letter stating, "You will get nothing", I was very angry. I understood the supposed core rules but felt that the "Last in, First out" was unfair. We all put money in. Evant put my money in without me even wanting it to. So we should all get a portion relative to the amount of money we put in.

As a CEO you can't actually just unilaterally sell a company. You have to get the investors to agree. How many investors? Well, it used to be *all* investors. Unanimous agreement. So my anger could have simply killed the acquisition. Evant would have been dead in the water because they couldn't convince me to agree to do something for "less than nothing".

Historically this rational rule turned out to be problematic. So some US States changed the rules and made corporate sales possible with simple majorities. But in exchange for this concession from investors, these States enable minority investors to "dissent". A dissenting investor will not block the sale, but will be able to get their money back because they don't want to participate in the sale. They don't want to be part of the new company that the majority is forcing them into.

So I wrote the people in charge a poignant email, and calculated what portion of the proceeds I should get given my percentage of investment dollars. Whomever I was communicating with wrote back and said something like "That isn't going to happen!" We may have conversed a few more times, with me clearly stating I was not going to agree to the sale, that I was dissenting, and that the law was pretty obvious on this. I believe the other side kept saying nothing was going to happen.

A few weeks later, an envelope came to me from Manhattan Associates. Inside it there was no letter or any form of explanation. But there was a check. A nicely sized check. I deposited it that day.

Love: Food

I have visited, but never lived in, New York City, but comparing the

cities I know fairly well (Philadelphia, Boston, San Francisco, and Los Angeles) the food scene in Los Angeles is on a completely different tier. I should correct that to say: the authentic ethnic food scene in Los Angeles is on a completely different tier. The reason is quite simple: Los Angeles is a vast area where different ethnic groups settle. Each group builds a mini-country in one or more parts of LA. Commonly these mini-countries are the largest populations of that ethnic group in the world, other than their original country. In their mini-countries in LA, they try to preserve their home country's culture as best they can, and they have so many people and so many resources that this preservation is quite easy. So there are dozens of countries magically crammed into the "tiny" metropolis of Los Angeles. But to get to them you need a key. You need a car.

My caravan always had at least two cars: my Toyota Celica and a Brunei Prince's Audi Quattro. Actually maybe he wasn't a prince; maybe he was simply the son of the doctor to the king of Brunei. But he was as arrogant as a prince. And as arrogant as me. And he had a better car. But having a car *at all* makes you elite in Los Angeles. Having a better car is just a footnote.

Chinese food was the top food of my caravan. We did frequent the Jewish deli called "Canters", enjoyed the dangerously bad hamburgers and chili of "Tommy's", and sometimes had Indian. But all these other culinary adventures were separated with one or more trips to Chinese food. I am not sure what caused the gravitation. We did have a fair amount of people of Chinese and Indian descent in our caravan. And I think that the combination of people ordering what they want, but everyone sharing and enjoying all the dishes, pushed Chinese and Indian to the top.

Maybe the final winning aspect for the Chinese food were the chopsticks.

Programming • point three

After going to the bottom (base two), and something akin to the top (base three-sixty), of the bases, we now return to our programming problem. What is the proper answer to 'A45'? Well, the language

of nibbles is "base-eight" and of course base-8 has no eights. The largest digit you have is a '7', so to get an eight, you need a '10', which I hope you no longer assume is a ten.

The base-eight answer to 'A45' is '11'. So the proper response to 'A45' is 'A4511'. This is definitely correct with the rules laid out so far, but it may be starting to make you feel uncomfortable. If 'A45' is 'A4511', that is great, but how do I add '45' to '11'? Wouldn't that be 'A4511'? But then how do I add '451' to '1'? Wouldn't that also be 'A4511'? How do I tell them apart? Unfortunately, you can't. And that leads us to a fun new word: "instruction size". And that new word makes us beg for many more queens. Women are critical to everything ☺

"Instruction size" is the number of nibbles that need to be read to understand what the "instruction" or action should be performed. All these instructions are part of what is called an Instruction Set, and that set of instructions defines all the rules for how a CPU works. It is the recipe book that CPU understands. So far, our CPU only understands 'A…', or one simple instruction. The "instruction size" of our CPU is (so far) a single nibble. It reads one card and from that it figures out what to do. If the card is an 'A' it adds the next two nibbles together, and the result of that is either one or two nibbles depending on the size of what was added. There is nothing wrong with what we have defined so far, except that 'A01' should not be 'A001'. Since we *might* need two nibbles for the answer, we might as well always have two nibbles for the answer. So 'A01' is 'A0001' and 'A44' is 'A4410'. The second being the equivalent of a 'ten' vs. a 'one'.

Five • point three

During the eighteen months or so, the Velidom team built a vision: a Software Factory where every developer was far more productive than they could ever be without the factory, where project managers could see hourly progress throughout the world, and where customers could see new versions of the product go live. It was a grand vision with lots of beautiful diagrams, interesting technology, novel and patentable solutions to problems, and an impressive

cluster of computers running in a data center. It was the perfect way to fail.

The Velidom product was too big to sell easily, and eighteen months was way too long to build a product without making sure it will sell. I had done some early sales work when the company launched, but as the company rolled along I was trapped trying to cover four roles that are very difficult to juggle. I should sell the product to customers, I should sell the company to investors, I should define the product for the development team, and finally, I should help build the product. The first three roles are not conflicting except that defining a product *in detail* is very time consuming and is unnecessary for sales. Juggling a bunch of rolls is not necessarily bad: you can always pause some activity as the other ones catch up. But the development team was independent of me, and the company effectively developed something before the company was sure what is should be trying to sell. That is a common "visionary product" problem for startups.

Car: The 110

Our food caravan always had at least two cars, and we would head out into the world of LA every few nights. At the time, the 210 freeway was relatively new and very little had been built along its corridor. So most of the city was either straight south of Pasadena or, more likely, somehow related to the heart of LA itself. To get to the heart of LA from Pasadena, you take the 110. It is called a freeway on most maps, but that is a misnomer. It is a raceway.

The 110 runs along the Arroyo Seco riverbed. There might be water in there, but I am not sure I ever saw any. Properly named. The important things about the 110 are: it is shaped like a river, it has three lanes, and it has stop-signs for onramps. LA roads in general have many more lanes than I experienced growing up. The big road into Philadelphia (the Schuykill Expressway) had only two lanes. Even crossing the country, seeing more than two lanes was uncommon. But LA roads like the 10 could have four or more. The 110 had the perfect number of lanes. Three lanes. Enough to avoid Parcheesi. Enough to dodge either right or left. The proper number

of lanes for a racetrack.

The 110 starts in Pasadena, so getting onto it from there is no problem. But all the other onramps are basically stop signs. You need to go from zero to sixty in ideally one second, but cars then and now don't work that way. So the racetrack frequently lost its rightmost lane because some ten-second acceleration was occurring there. This was a feature of the racetrack. Like in a video game where part of the track shoots flames at you.

Parcheesi in racing is where two (idiot) cars travel at exactly the same speed right next to each other. It is amongst the worse sins in car driving. Either go faster, or go slower, or simply go behind the other car. All of these provide space for cars going much faster than you to get through. Having three lanes made the 110 relatively immune to Parcheesi. Having the stop-sign onramps made it completely inoculated.

So to race on the 110 you are primarily choosing between the left lane (the proper fast lane), and the right lane. Normal traffic is in the middle lane. While twisting back and forth with the riverbed, you are constantly looking at the right lane to figure out if it is the faster lane for this brief moment. Is it worth the double-lane switch?

It was a blast.

Love: Commitment

I can't say I can explain *why* I was so committed to Rebecca from the first day I met her. There was just something compelling about her. I wanted to be with her. I had no idea what I would do when I was with her. But I loved playing hearts with her on Catalina. I loved eating dinner with her in Los Angeles. We were not alone during these events; there were plenty of other people I liked to hang out with. But I always wanted her to be there too. When a glomming pack formed around her, I would always be there. The difference between me and the other glommers is that I would *never* leave. I believe I was nice, and maybe interesting, and maybe attractive. Those are just beliefs, which you can confirm or deny with Rebecca

herself. But *I know* I was committed. I was totally committed, to her.

Maybe Rebecca appreciated that commitment, either consciously or subconsciously. The glomming packs eventually dispersed, and it was only Rebecca & me, and our mutual friends. And sometimes it was just the two of us, alone. Rebecca and I argued a lot. But that wasn't a problem, it was just a part of our relationship. I was very happy.

Five • point four

When you have a potentially unsellable product but have not put in that much time to sell it, you have two paths. Try to sell the product, or "pivot" and try to build and sell a different product. Well, you actually have a third path but no entrepreneur ever sees it. You can shutdown. Whether ten thousand dollars or millions of dollars, there is a point that any additional time and money will not recover the situation. This is actually pretty easy for others with experience to see: you simply look at the value of the assets of the company and compare it to the expense to get to that value. If the value is much less than the expense, the company is probably hopeless. Velidom had a lot of assets (computer hardware and intellectual property) but the expense to get there was large and the value of the assets was unclear. But I never even thought about this formula. We had invested so much time and money in the company that I had to make it work.

Not knowing which path was better, I bet on both. I would try to sell the current product. We would start providing services to cover employee expenses. And I would try to come up with a slightly different product that was easier to sell. Investing in three paths makes each less likely to succeed, but hedges your bets.

Family: Koi

Koi are beautiful, large, goldfish. Koi means "carp" in Japanese, and it is also a homophone with another word that means "love".

Rebecca, Maya, and Katrina are my Koi.

Unfortunately, my Koi live in an aquarium that has an open drain. It is a beautiful aquarium with many wonderful things in it. The food is amazing and the schools exceptional. Only the ornamental house is a bit run down. And my Koi are beautiful, healthy, and happy fish. The water is always fresh and clean, because dirty water pours out the open drain. Replenishing fresh water gets poured in the top, every month. Usually.

How we came to be in The Slums of Palo Alto is a progression of our Slumlord raising the rent repeatedly, so the open drain became bigger and bigger. The drain was a reasonable size when we first moved into Palo Alto. But the relentless rent increases meant more and more gallons of water would pour out the drain every month. This was problem one.

Problem two was that I did my own startup (Velidom), which drained our cash reserves severely. There was a point where Velidom was clearly failing but I still needed to pay employees and other company expenses. Our family's reserves were all but flushed away.

These experiences then lead to problem three: After Velidom, I did a series of startups to try to get better at the engineering execution side. Most of these startups behaved reasonably and lawfully towards employees. We would negotiate a salary, which would be less than what I wanted but "survivable". And we would negotiate a stock percentage, which would ultimately be irrelevant because the stock was destined to be worthless. As the rent kept increasing, the startup salaries became less clearly survivable. But I somehow managed to string them all together and keep the aquarium running fairly well. There was a huge toll on me, but generally the younger Koi had no idea.

Then we get to a "not nice" startup. With this startup, I had an employment agreement that gave me about ten gallons of water a month after taxes. This was a very low salary (the lowest ever post-Velidom), but the charter of the company and the possibility of

helping others excited me. The aquarium was draining ten gallons a month normally, but sometimes more like twelve. This was not an ideal situation, but draining a net gallon a month is not catastrophic. And maybe the startup has potential, will get better funded, and I can renegotiate up to twelve or fourteen gallons a month.

Then the "not nice" kicks in. About a year in, suddenly my paystub is *half* what it was. I believe there was some mention of cash-flow issues, which I have some empathy for, but employees are supposed to be protected from these kinds of issues. You would think the employer would just lay me off, but the issue with the smallest stages of startups is some people are not optional.

Math • point three

There is another way to have a base larger than ten. You can have multiple "units" that are different quantities of smaller "units". The world is primarily divided into "Imperial" vs. "Metric" units, with a few other units scattered into the equation. For example, there are four quarts in a gallon and a thousand grams in a kilogram. The imperial units came about through practicality and a long history of "need to call it something". They seem byzantine compared to the metric system, but they are far more natural. How long is a foot? It is about the length of a foot. How many inches in a foot? Twelve.

The metric people say "That is weird" but I say "that is *right*". There is no reason to have units be based on ten. Ten is a *horrible* number. It is divisible by two and five. How many times have you needed to divide a sandwich by five? Or much of anything by five? Very unlikely. More likely is three or four or even six. Oh wait. Twelve is divisible by two, three, four, and six. And what is smaller than an inch? Basically nothing but fractions of inches. Like half, quarter, eighth, and twelfth.

The metric systems decimal scale model makes absolutely no sense as a human-usable system. It is difficult to divide and loses accuracy or precision on every division. But a crazy committee wanted to standardize on some base, and they picked base-ten. In

spite of there being a well-know, and world-wide better base. Not exactly base-twelve, but go check the time.

Yes, we use base-twelve and the even more precise base-sixty all the time. By the time you get to base-sixty, you are divisible by two, three, four, five, six, ten, twelve, fifteen, twenty, and thirty. That is a lot of ways to slice something. Seconds into minutes. Minutes into hours. Hours into days. A day has a lot of seconds in it, but it is a very natural progression up the unit scale. We even have an extra precise base-360 for degrees.

Five • point five

Investing in the three different paths yielded some interest in Velidom 1.0 (the software factory), Velidom 2.0 (a virtual desktop environment), and Velidom 3.0 (an online music system). But the interest was never enough for me to get investment. During these product and audience pivots, I would continue to have no salary and be running a significant computer expense. When I shut down the data center is when Velidom curbed its primary expense.

It took years to kill the actual company: we had a possibly valuable patent, a bunch of intellectual property, and computers. But Velidom is now officially dead in Delaware, where it was incorporated. Rebecca helped me put it down.

Fini Five

Right: Vision

Getting the right vision for a startup is critical. Later I will discuss [[TBD]] ….

Wrong: Experience

My biggest failure with Velidom was simply not recognizing (before launch) that without a particular set of partners I was missing critical skills. I had advisors to help out, but I needed days or months of

work from someone with years of experience. Customer sales and fund raising were textbook familiar to me, but were not something I had ever had to do outside software consulting. I was not experienced and needed someone who was.

This is the core problem of an overly visionary startup. Visions can appear to live independently of a company or customers. It is a beautiful vision. Even making the vision into a product doesn't solve the core issue: who are you helping, what are you helping them with, and what is that worth to them? The other kinds of startups are a bit safer: beat the big company on price in an existing market or slice out a high-end piece of an existing market. Visions commonly believe a new market will emerge. And you need a very experienced person to quickly confirm or deny that belief with actual customers and funding sources.

Kindness: Jewelry

About the same time as when I started this book, it dawned on me that Rebecca and I had been together for quite some time. A total of thirty years. Thirty years of monogamous companionship. I wouldn't call it 'bliss', especially in the first decade, but I love her dearly and strive to work through any issue between us to continue to be together. To make her happy. Thirty years is quite a bit of time. Spend it well and it can provide a lot of depth and love in your life.

By nature I am a pretty modest guy. No bling on my person. Rebecca is also a modest woman. We live in an area where a lot of people show off their wealth, but because we both (a) have no wealth and (b) don't like to show off, we look like very simple people. Every weekday I wear a polo shirt and black pants from Macy's. Pretty sure most of America could buy and where my daily uniform. On weekends, I wear a shirt saying 'Wizard'. Pretty sure most of America could afford that too.

But again, this year is special. Thirty years together with a person you love is an amazing event. I want to celebrate it. But how?

Every Christmas I wander the nearby mall to get inspiration. By the time of this book, I know the salespeople very well, and they know me and my habits. But for most of the years I wandered this mall, I was just some balding older white person looking intensely at the cases inside their store. I might sometimes ask a simple question or two. And then I would wander away.

I felt bad when I traipsed through the mall this way, but I also recognized two things (a) I had to do this to figure out what I was going to buy, and (b) lots of other people wander through without buying. Being in retail can be an excruciatingly frustrating job. You are not in control of your daily income. You are a slave to the buyers. You "need to" make the sale, they simply "want to" make a purchase.

Again, the year of this book happens to be Rebecca and my thirtieth anniversary. That is a pretty notable event. It is also a year we are clearly not in the slums any more. The rent is the same (actually higher) but we have a new landlord that is a bit more reasonable and is likely to give us a bit more notice if they want the house back. And my earnings are now large enough to have buffers again, so we can find alternative housing with more flexibility.

So this year, I want to give Rebecca something pretty special. We live a modest life with little in terms of jewelry or other visible wealth. I like that, but also want Rebecca to feel special. To have her know that I love her dearly and love that we have a life and family together.

Our anniversary is officially in September, but before Mother's day I am wandering the mall. Trying to put an idea together. Trying to make sure I can afford it. And then 'C' comes to my aid, in an amazing way.

Ultimately I decided to buy Rebecca a set of baubles that represented our family. One item for each of us. I thought this was a neat idea, and I would actually time it so one represented Rebecca's birth, one my joining her life, and one for each of our daughters when they joined her (our) life. But the numbers were not good. They were about 25% higher than I could reasonable muster the

money for.

So I studied the retailers to see if they had any sales, and maybe I could get the items on sale. Some retailers don't have discounts or sales. Their cash registers can't even process the concept. Made me sad because the sales people were so helpful, but such is life.

Fortunately the primary contender for my purchase clearly does have sales. They were periodically listed on their Facebook page. And when I asked 'C' about getting things on sale, she said "I love sales! And I will help you!" That is definitely a promising thing to hear, so I was hopeful to get the 25% off. And I did on two of the items (she bought them for me during a "Trunk Sale"). But the other two items didn't qualify for that sale. Instead, about three months after I talked with 'C' and without any required effort on my part, two more items were picked up. For 33% off.

I now visit 'C' almost every month to check in with her, and to thank her for her help. An amazingly nice person. Very skilled with fashion too ☺

School

155
STOP

SIX

After the failure that was Velidom, I decided I really needed to learn how to do startups. I had five under my belt, but wanted to learn from someone who had succeeded before. A friend from Evant had connections into the gaming industry, and a casual, social, gaming company was looking for a server engineer. I interviewed and did quite well. The company was Winster.

Winster was founded by Jerry Kaplan, who was the founder of GO in the 1980s. GO was a very notable startup in it's success, pricey acquisition, and ultimate crash within AT&T. Jerry had made a lot of people a lot of money and eventually retired. He re-entered the startup world out of boredom, which is a somewhat unusual motivator. But his history and his book made him a very credible person to learn from. And I learned a lot from him and Winster.

Startups: Death

Startups die. The death of a startup is a hard thing for many people, but it is insanely hard for a founder. As a founder it truly feels like you gave birth to your company. You raised it for at least two years. It is a toddler or maybe a teenager. And it is dying. Worse than that. It is dying and *you* are responsible for putting it down.

I have helped others keep companies alive until they were sold. And I have watched startups die after I have left. But the terminal illness of Velidom was so hard for me to accept that I basically denied it died at all. Even to today. It is my car's license plate.

Because employees are 'protected' it is the founder's responsibility to make sure the death of a startup does not poorly impact them. Employees should have a good heads-up so they can find new jobs, and their final wages and PTO should be paid. But the character of the CEO and the strain of the death of his child can make them behave badly.

There was a woman who was in a company that was clearly terminal. The product was going nowhere. The market was going nowhere. They were making less and less money from fewer and fewer people. The CEO didn't believe in pivoting[48]. There was no more money. There was absolutely no hope.

One day this woman came to talk to me and asked me for advice. She had been offered a position at a large gaming startup down in Sunnyvale. She was to be some kind of team lead, where currently she was just an individual programmer. Or more accurately, she was the *only* programmer because the company could no longer afford more than one. She was lonely and wanted colleagues to learn from. But her current CEO/founder kept telling her how important she was to him and the company. How the company could make a turnaround, and she would be a critical part of that. So she asked me what she should do.

I told her *exactly* what I thought she should do. It is exactly what I would do in her shoes. I also explained to her what I wrote above. The company is the founder's baby. The baby is all but dead. This particular founder only really responded to assertive, forceful, and even aggressive actions positively. And now the founder was suffering from delusions… of life… in a baby… because it is his baby. I explained to her that I know I suffered from the same delusions with Velidom. I do not believe I hurt any employees in the process, and I am not the same kind of person as her founder. But I have complete empathy for him. And if I received the offer she had. I would high tail it away from him (or from me) as fast as I could.

So that was my advice to her. Take the offer. As fast as you can. And given I was in a gaming startup at the time, I knew a fair amount about what other gaming startups were out there. So I guessed which one she might have been given an offer by, that happened to be located in Sunnyvale. I told her if it was *that company*, she should run even faster. She did not tell me that I was correct until years later.

---

[48] Pivoting: Changing company and product direction based on gaining better knowledge of the target market

The woman did not take my advice and continued working for the dead baby. This was unfortunate in many ways. Unfortunate because the new company and position would likely have been good for her: having colleagues is an emotional and educational blessing. And unfortunate because I think she could have used the money. If they offered her just 0.1% equity, she could have bought something nice. Like a house. With cash. The company was Playfish.

Commitment: More and Less

A saying at Caltech was "At MIT you learn less and less about more and more, until you know nothing about everything. At Caltech you learn more and more about less and less, until you know everything about nothing." Basically representing the choices between generalization and specialization. You only have so much time, so you have to pick. Techers[49] picked the latter. I am not sure whether MIT students agreed with the stereotyping. But I do know that making either choice is a box.

The right phrase is "I want to learn more and more about more and more, until I know everything about everything". Time, the whims of DNA, and wayward busses will prevent ultimate achievement, but *that goal* should be your goal.

As of this time, I know approximately thirty-six computer-programming languages. I am fluent in at least a dozen of them, and professionally competent in the rest. If you offer me a job that requires any one of the thirty-six, and I accept the job, you will likely be very happy with my productivity. I am a polyglot: a programmer who can program in many languages. Many different types of languages. Very quickly and effectively.

This was not easy to accomplish, and was not true for me thirty-five years ago. Back then I could program in two languages at best: BASIC and 6502 assembly language. But with thirty-five years of

---

[49] Techer: A person matriculating through the undergraduate portion of Caltech. Caltech Graduate schools were a bit different.

perseverance I became fluent and competent at more and more of the great and useful computer languages created. My ability to translate customer (your) needs into well-structured computer programs became exceptional, whatever the language I was using. "More and more about more and more".

I entered the computer world during the golden era for programmers. Computers had finally reached a price point where normal people could own one (if painful) and normal people could *understand* one.

In the golden era, you could open the machine up and look at its parts. See a CPU. See the RAM. See the connection to the keyboard, screen, joystick, and other peripherals. A layer down, you could look at the circuits in the CPU and see registers, adders, etc. A layer up, you could see the assembly language that the computer (the CPU) understood. See the language that talked to the keyboard, screen, joystick, etc. At first, it is not easy to understand how that CPU thinks. But back then, it doesn't think very much, so getting into its head is pretty easy if you make the effort. Next you wander up to Basic. Now you are no longer getting into the head of the computer. You are trying to become fluent in a language that is easier for *your head* to understand. It will later be translated into Assembly and Machine Code by something called a compiler.

Almost nothing has really changed between then and now, except everything has grown and shrunk. All in ways that hurt the human ability to comprehend computers. CPUs are much more complicated. A 6502 had about four thousand transistors. The Apple A7 has a billion. Assembly language has a similar kind of structure, but is maybe four times as complicated. GPUs[50] are added into the mix with the CPU. And the plethora of languages that "make programming easier" for humans is in the dozens. Much more stuff. And all the physical stuff you want to see has shrunken to be basically invisible to a human. An iPhone is smaller than the 8K memory expansion card for an Atari computer.

---

[50] Graphical Processing Units, able to do calculations in mass so your photorealistic video game can show more than thirty frames per second

I am amazed that kids today can grok computers at all. I do my best to help them understand things bit by bit, but it is not an easy task. The internet helps.

Homes: Motor

Compared to Mobile Homes, Motor Homes are totally awesome in pretty much every way imaginable. Motor Homes are sometimes called RVs (for Recreation Vehicles), but that is a misnomer for the truly awesome MH. A fun RV can sleep two to four people, might have some kind of sink and maybe some kind of stove, and can nicely move down the road at 60 MPH and maybe 15 MPG. That is definitely fun, but it is not awesome.

A MH is not a vehicle first, it is a *home* first. Or at least a house first, with the home-ness provided by the occupants. To be a MH you must (a) have bathrooms, a kitchen, and beds, (b) be able to have a *mortgage* because this is clearly a house not just a financeable vehicle, and (c) be able to move within a few minutes notice. Note that the movement is last. If English were a bit more eloquent, the MH would become an HM and stand for a "House, most mobile".

Because we live in the Slums of Palo Alto, the first house we will ever own, the first property we will ever have a mortgage for, is likely to be: a house, most mobile.

Boxes: Mavvi

The CIO at "Mavvi" (a large retailer) invited two colleagues and me to help Mavvi improve its development processes, and potentially to help it replace weak team members and recruit better ones. Because my two colleagues and I had worked together quite closely over the years, we were very friendly and comfortable with each other. At some point, people called us "The Three Amigos" and the name stuck. My two colleagues were product and program managers and basically nontechnical. So I was the engineering Amigo. I love helping companies improve themselves, and the whole initiative of Mavvi's "Stratus" program was compelling.

I dove into the project with relish: I met maybe a hundred different developers, saw all the tools and processes they used (they varied between different teams), and looked through the source code itself. During this period I also looked at the "Point Of Sale" software that was currently running in the stores. Sadly I may have been one of the only software engineers that had a running cash register on my laptop, plus the source code to see how it worked.

After about a week, I had started my list of recommendation. During the last decade I had repeatedly evolved and refined what the best tools were, and Mavvi was in the same technology space (Java-based) as most of my startups were. So my recommendations were very mainstream, and very well tested. They were used at my last startup, and that team was humming along very productively.

The one thing missing from my recommendation was any statement about personnel. I had observed various personnel issues, but until you have a reasonable process and culture, you can't blame the people. So I didn't, I was making purely process and tool recommendations. A total of twenty recommendations. I was later to hear it became called "Mark's Manifesto". Hah.

Mavvi has lots of little fiefdoms. Each fiefdom has a lord of the fief, and with that great title comes a mighty axe. For each of my very mainstream, very effective, very tested recommendations there was a lord who swung his might axe and destroyed it. Twenty recommendations, twenty axes, and behold the manifesto has been put in its place.

Apparently the Mavvi team liked me if not my recommendations, because they asked me to stay and join them in their little box. I declined. I don't like boxes in general, and this one felt more like a coffin.

Programming: Assembly

Assembly language is not really a different language from Machine Language: the semantics of Assembly language are identical to the

ML it is based on, or at least it has very little augmentation in that regard. The only change is that the rules of your card game become manifest in the labels of all those nibbles. Instead of having a '1', which in a particular context means 'add two nibbles and put the result right after them' in your language, the assembly version would be a nice name like 'Add2PutAfter'. So the quite obscure sequence of '145' in machine language would now nicely be 'Add2PutAfter,4,5;' or something similar.

Now that you can program in the one true language, programming in assembly is a breeze. Just take out some note cards and on the unlined side, write things like '1' or even '35' if you started having a lot more instructions, and then on the lined side write a nice short name, and maybe even an expanded explanation beneath it. Now any time you have a nibble like a '1' as an instruction, you can put the equivalent note card in its place. If you have a nibble pair like '35', you do the same.

Voila! You are still one with the matrix, but have a somewhat easier mental burden. You have also learned your first *great* programming language. The biggest flaw with both Machine Language and Assembly Language to us humans is that they aren't one language each. They are dozens of languages, actually hundreds of languages, each distinct because each CPU (each Machine) is distinctly different and has its own language.

So knowing ML and AL for a given Machine is definitely knowing the Machine very intimately. That is wonderful. But knowing hundreds of machines intimately is a bit tiring. So computer scientists and lesser skilled computer people come up with their own "higher level" languages. These sacrifice intimacy for human productivity. Sometimes the sacrifices are too great and the programming language inane. But all the great programming languages have incredible benefits for the modest (or large) sacrifices they make.

Six • point two

Winster was originally trying to be a gambling site: you could win

real money by playing the Winster games, which were a lot like casino games. This first incarnation failed the legality test at the time, so Winster had morphed into a site where you could win prizes by accumulating certain number of points in the games. It was a subscription model as the primary revenue source: you could play for a while and then you had to pony up your credit card. Getting people through that "paywall" was the core optimization that Jerry was focused on.

There are a few different kinds of startup founders. Some have a clear product vision and then try to achieve it and sell it. That is "inventing the future". Some have a clearly defined problem and try to solve that through customer interaction. Which is more like "solving the now". And there are founders who can make products that are less expensive than what already exists. These are optimizers. They are very good at making things less expensive and more efficient than current products. things run more cheaply than they do already. So a phrase "Not new, but cheaper!"

Car: Fast and Steady

There is a saying: "Slow and steady wins the race". This is a lie. Fast and steady win races. Fast and steady with a breakaway in the home stretch. Just watch California Chrome.

The two best cars in our Caltech food caravan were my 1982 Toyota Celica and the 1982 Audi Quattro. The Quattro gets its name from having four-wheel drive. It had a better engine, better transmission, and better suspension than my Celica. It was a superior race vehicle.

The initial 110 raceway runs against the Quattro proved how much better the Quattro and it's driver were. You can make a lot of mistakes on the 110: Going right and being trapped by a stop-sign car. Going left and being Parcheesied. The Quattro was able to recover from these mistakes very easily. So all the initial runs on the 110 raceway went to it, because it was clearly superior.

Driving fast on LA freeways, including the 110, is all about steadiness. Yes, if you have a Maserati, you can pretend you are driving fast just about any way you like. But "you" are not driving fast, your car is fast. And it is common to see fast Maserati's that are trapped because of an idiotically slow driver.

LA freeways have many lanes filled with cars driving at all kinds of different speeds. At any time of day where racing is possible, the lanes themselves tend to have relatively consistent speeds (say 70 MPH for the left lane), and they also have spaces. Some are large spaces, where a car is very much ahead of the trailing car. Some are small spaces, because even just a one-second rule[51] at 70 MPH produces 50 feet of space. To drive fast in LA, you wander the spaces. Ideally wandering the least amount, but wandering is better than accelerating and braking. If you get good at wandering, you don't brake at all. You fly.

For about six months the Quattro punished my poor Celica and me. But eventually I learned to fly. And the better engine, transmission, and suspension of the Quattro were meaningless. The 'quattro' was meaningless. We weren't in the desert, but on LA freeways. And both cars were flying. Wins were a toss-up.

Six • point three

Winster had a small team of developers who were trying to make new games, optimize the paywall, interact with PayPal, handle marketing campaigns, and various other new functionality. But the architecture for the Winster product was built at the wrong time… by the wrong person… Winster was using Java, which is a reasonable technology at its core, but has gone down a number of bad paths over the years. Winster was using one of its bad paths (call Java Server Pages) for a lot of what Winster was doing. Winster was also using a technology called Flex from Adobe. Flex was a language on top of Flash and when I joined Winster, it was a very

---

[51] A rule of being at least one-second behind the car ahead. For safety we drivers are supposed to use a two-second rule, and for all new drivers out there, please use the two-second rule. But in LA, any two-second space will promptly be occupied by between one and four cars

good technology. Except that was Flex 2.0 and Winster was built in Flex 1.0. Flex 1.0 was a horribly convoluted and bizarre technology. Both of these "had to go" while still meeting the deadlines for other activities and not breaking the current running web site and games.

Swapping out technology is unfortunately a very large and onerous task. You almost never can do it piecemeal efficiently. If you are not sure about a new technology, you can do a pilot of a part of the system. And sometimes you can migrate new things to new technology and leave the old things in the old technology. That makes the old 'brittle' but if it can eventually be turned off, then it is not a problem.

The part I like about swapping out technology: it usually punishes you very clearly when done as a big-bang. You swap, you try it out, everything is broken, and you start over. Having a cataclysmic failure is much better than a plethora of subtle issues. If you get fast enough at iterating, you eventually have *no failure* and likely *few issues* because the lack of failure shows you really understood the problem completely.

This benefit of cataclysmic failure is visible in a lot of sports. Golf is so brutal to mistakes that when you can finally swing at full-energy and hit the ball "mostly right", your shot is going to fly very nicely. The intolerance of the club-head becomes the reward of the flight.

Family: Western, Eastern, Atomic • point two

I have been a part of both my Western family and Eastern family for many decades. Early on, it seemed like my Western family had a clear advantage of history and supposed similarity to me for getting my attention and "affection". But they would prove those were no advantages at all, and as time progressed many of the westerners would shrink their atoms to not include me, or would refuse to join the super-atom that was my home. Or they had lives that made having families difficult in every way. Or simply very unfortunate fate.

In any case, I can confidently say that I have four incredibly strong families: our "home", my parents' tiny atomic family, the Chen clan, and the Shen clan. Our family is a strong member, destined to be much stronger, to all of these. I also have weak families based off my Western grandmothers "Grand Mary" and "Granny Kay", but it is unclear where those families will go in the future.

The Chen clan is based off Rebecca's maternal grandmother: Rebecca's mother was the only daughter so the rest of the family is related to Rebecca by five uncles. Most of the Chen clan lives in Taiwan, so they are the major "to the west of us" force. Chen's are very loving, and they made sure their widowed sister and her family had a good home somewhere, even after emigration to the United States.

The Shen clan is also very loving, but in contrast, it is *everywhere.* Seattle, Rochester, DC, Taiwain, LA, San Francisco, and the list goes on and on. Geography has no effect on Shen mobility. Rebecca's father was the first son in the Shen clan, and I believe the third or fourth child. In total, there were three boys and six girls. And pretty much every single child was intellectually amazing. And pretty much every one of these amazing children married an amazing spouse. And that produced amazing children. If we enumerate the occupations of the Shen clan, it includes lawyers, doctors, educators with doctorates, and at the lowly bottom engineers without doctorates. In that regard, Rebecca and I are near the bottom. But because we believe in Family so much, we are working our way up. We will ultimately overcome our lack of credentials.

Six • point four

Winster had two technologies that need to change: (a) Flex 1.0 pages have to be converted to Flex 2.0 and (b) JSP pages have to be converted to something better. The team knew this for months before I showed up. They knew it was killing their ability to deliver new things. That if *they just did it,* they would be rewarded. But month after month it never happened.

Velidom cost me, my family, and my friends a lot of money and energy. Velidom did not make me a better CEO. Or minimally so. It did not make me a better fund-raiser or sales-person. Or minimally so. But it did make me a better executioner. If something needs to be built in software, computer hardware, or through online services, I knew I could do it. Quickly and effectively.

Within the first month, I transformed the Winster code base. The other developers would leave on a Friday afternoon. I would spend all weekend transforming the code to a new version. By Monday morning everything would be working. Each weekend, something transformed. Monday was always the deadline to make sure it did not interfere with the normal working week. My coworkers with happy and impressed.

Jerry was also happy and impressed. One night Jerry came to visit me in Palo Alto, and after a long walk around the blocks of Leland Manor, I became the Vice President, Engineering of Winster reporting directly to him. I jumped up two rungs in the organization and was now the boss of my boss.

Koi • point two

Why couldn't I be fired? Can't anyone be fired pretty easily? Well, not if you are desperately needed. And in startups you commonly don't have the money and the time to create redundant positions. Some people are needed all the time until you find a replacement person or team. I am commonly in this position for a while, which is fiscally good for the company but also risky if I am "lost".

For this company, I ran *all* of the production systems[52]. Even more, all these systems were all run *on my accounts*. My credit card was being billed. If they fired me, everything would shut down in a single phone call. Further, I am the only one who could maintain all these systems and their software. I had written all the code that

---

[52] Production systems are the computers that customers interact with. If you google something, you are hitting Google's production servers. As compared to say Apple's internal mail systems.

customers were paying to use. The company could not afford any more software developers. They basically couldn't afford me. I was later to find out that they had only enough money to fund my four-year employment contract for exactly one year. And had no intention of putting any more money in. So when they ran out of money, they couldn't fire me. But they could 'short' me. And that is what they did.

So back to my precious Koi. The aquarium is draining at ten gallons a month, and I am abruptly filling it at five gallons a month. This is a serious problem. You could say I should move to a different aquarium, but this is mid-school-year when this happens. Changing aquariums would be difficult (most aquariums open up in the summer), and we can't legally leave Palo Alto while the kids are in school here. Further, changing aquariums loses a lot of water. You have to rent the new aquarium, which has its own drain. And then moving the Koi to the new aquarium causes more gallons to spill into someone else's aquarium. So moving was not really an option.

I had to figure out how to get more water. My only resources were my particular skills, and the fact that no startup that is shorting you can expect you to work eighty hours a week. So I now had forty hours a week to save my Koi.

Six • point five

For many months, things with Winster went really well. We built a Facebook like profile page for players. We added new games every month instead of every quarter. We fixed the data center and network issues. And we had much better analytics on player behavior. The development team was happy and doing good work.

Then things got a little strange. Games people built were not released and although we had a prototype that integrated with Facebook (about the same time as Zynga) it was never released. Jerry did not believe Winster customers would use Facebook. Jerry did not believe Winster customers would like a game like Sudoku. As part of my growth in working in or with startups, I eventually grew

to simply accepting these decisions. The founder / CEO of a startup *owns* the idea of the startup. They own the product. I can make suggestions if I have background in the area the startup is in. I can offer advise if asked. But it is *their* company and they must choose what they want to do with it.

So I simply "quit" Winster. I told Jerry there was not enough product work to have me there full time. The existing developers could continue all the things he needed from the product. And we could have a retained part-time contract to make sure if anything broke or required a lot of effort, I was available.

Fini Six

Right: Technology

With a few minor fixes, Winster had a great technology stack. It wasn't great in a completely universal way, but it was thoroughly solving the needs of the Winster product. It made the customers happy. We added new features that made customers even more happy every release cycle. It was rare for Winster to have production issues, and the worse production issue was caused by an incompetent IT person and not the core technology of Winster.

Picking the right technology for a given product is not an easy thing. Technology is constantly moving, and picking something stupid (e.g. Flex 1.0) may actually be betting on the right technology a little early (e.g. Facebook) and ultimately have a big win. But if you have a decent product for your customers' needs, you should generally error pretty conservatively with the technology. What are you *sure* will be good enough, vs. what *may* be even better but you have not used it yet.

If early customers are happy, you can always make them happier by migrating to something better after you figure out their needs.

Wrong: Customer

You can have the completely wrong customer for your desired product. If you are making electric cars and you target too broad a market, you will never find a price-point that matches your customers abilities. Similarly, Winster was targeting customers that were so under-employed that they could spend all night playing the equivalent of slot-machines. Yes, your product appeals to them, but neither they nor any marketing company is willing to spend any significant amount of money.

A different problem is targeting a particularly unique company. When Evant targeted Staples as a customer, we could hone into the problems that Staples had, which is dealing with thousands of stores carrying tens of thousands of products. But the number of companies out there that have that kind of problem is relatively small. So your product better produce a lot of income per sale (potentially from services) or you will never have a profitable product line.

Kindness: Commissions

I mentioned before that I commonly wander showrooms and even (in the case of Mobile Homes) may spend several hours discussing products with sales people. That might seem quite the imposition on them for a "possible sale", but I am a pretty friendly (even interesting) guy so salespeople don't seem to mind spending time with me. Further, a critical characteristic of me as a purchaser is that I reward people's time. The commission *always* goes to who ever spent the time with me. In recent years I strongly stepped up my name-recall and this was part of the reason. If 'R' helps me pick out a suit, then 'R' will get the commission. Not somebody else in their department, and not Amazon.

This would seem obvious behavior for anyone obeying "The Golden Rule": do unto others as you would have others due unto you. An even better version is Rawl's "Veil of Ignorance" as a way to determine true justice and fairness. With Rawl's Veil, you must

identify the two (or more) possible roles in a particular situation. Say one is as a "Suit Buyer" and one is as a "Suit Seller". The two spend an hour going over suits. And then the "Suit Buyer" either buys from the Seller or someone else (say an online store). So how do you decide which is fair? Well, what if you *don't know* which role you are in? You could be the Buyer or the Seller? You don't know. It is Veiled from you. Wouldn't that make you do the only thing that is truly right and fair? Give yourself as seller the commission because you deserve it. And make yourself as buyer pay for the time and expertise they took from the seller.

Which ever role you are in, you see the outcome as fair.

SEVEN

"Always Google the CEO." That is one of my recommendations for deciding whether to work for a startup, and for knowing what you are getting into if you choose to join. Startups in their young years are a pure reflection of the CEO and whatever "right hand" (or first lieutenant) the CEO has. Yes, there can be cofounders who provide spirit to the company, and these can certainly flavor the environment. And catalysts can do a lot to the environment too. But if the CEO or his "hand" want things to go a certain way, then they definitely will. So make sure you find out as much as possible about these people before you start. Take the interviews very seriously: you are interviewing a company to figure out what that company is really like. Ask nicely and the employees will commonly tell you many interesting things. They may tell you things that very much affect your decisions.

A coworker at 'seven' has a different recommendation from mine. His is: "Never work for a convicted felon". Combining the two might avoid you much grief.

Switching to consulting for Winster was very financially lucrative. Winster clearly needed my help, and my hourly rate times the number of hours they needed me produced reasonable income. But the CEO of Winster was an optimizer, so bit by bit he was trying to get my billable hours down further and further. I clearly needed a better long-term prospect.

I found it in an 'arrogance meets arrogance' battle. A company was offering the thirteenth employee position to someone who could do either 'A' or 'B' or 'C'. After all the things I did for Winster, I knew very well how to do everything that were enumerated, I called myself (for the first time) an "Engineering Tour de Force" and told them I could do all of 'A', 'B', and 'C'. Three positions: I could do them all. I ultimately got the thirteen employee mug as swag from a company called FooMojo. The number turned out to be very accurate for 'seven' (FooMojo) was a cursed ride.

Programming • point four

So far our programming has all been in the small. Talking directly to the computer to get it to do something for us. Programming sometimes works that way, and sometimes works the opposite: from the human problem into the details of how to explain the problem and solution to a computer. When you are working outside in, you are really working from the human model into a good computer model. And how you think makes a lot of difference.

There are many paradigms to thinking about problems in a human solvable way, but probably the most interesting and intelligible contrast is between "Classic Imperative" and "Object-Oriented" programming. So far, we have been giving commands to a computer. That is "imperative". We give it a command, it tells us an answer. We save the answer and give it another command.

This works quite well in the small, but can cause you programs to become very hard to understand as they become bigger and bigger. They may work, but there are too many details to understand the bigger pictures. It is like instead of seeing your pet, his eyes, and her tail, you see every last detail of your pet all together. That is a very overwhelming vision.

A great, incredibly short, and powerful explanation for how Smalltalk and Object-Oriented programming is different from classic programming is a book called "A Taste of Smalltalk" by Ted Kaehler and Dave Patterson. I loved the paradigm so much that I translated it to Ruby, Scratch, and Flex. But I recommend the original unless you know one of these other languages, in which case I still recommend the original but you might read my version too ☺.

"A Taste of Smalltalk" starts with a simple problem: program a computer to solve the Towers of Hanoi. The Towers of Hanoi is a puzzle where you have a stack of discs on one of three poles. The discs get progressively smaller as you get higher in the stack. You goal is to move the tower from one pole to another while obeying two major rules: (a) move one disc at a time, and (b) bigger discs can't be on top of smaller discs [or they squash them].

To keep things brief, the classic solution involves a core algorithm of 'moveTower' that calls 'moveDisc' and 'moveTower' recursively. The data of where the discs are is initially stored within parameters. Later the disc data is moved outside parameters (so we can see progress along the way) but then they become part of some global-like state shared by the core algorithm. This is very classic, with a strong program vs. data separation and algorithms that make sense to programmers but have certain critical issues inherent to them. The object-oriented solution flips things around a bit to get rid of the issues.

If you consider the Towers of Hanoi, can you imagine anything about the puzzle that would make it much easier? For example, in Harry Potter's Wizard Chess, the pieces know how to move. You can tell them what to do, but you can't tell them to move incorrectly. This would be quite handy in learning to play chess. Similarly, for the Towers, what if the pieces *knew the rules?* Even better, what if the pieces *loved* the rules. They loved them so much that they know: what their best move is (if any), and how to move onto their best move. Then the core program of Towers of Hanoi would be incredibly simple:

- Find the next disc that has a legal move
- Ask that disc to move onto that legal destination
- No moving the same disc twice in a row

That is it.

Whether the discs are barely more than number holders, or cool animated graphics, the algorithm is the same. And whether there are five discs or five hundred, the algorithm is the same for both the tower and to the discs. You have isolated the internals of disc behavior, what discs can rightly understand what to do, from the external desires placed on the discs. This is called in Object-Oriented Programming, encapsulation. It is sometimes called "hiding", but it isn't hiding to prevent you from getting to something important. Smalltalk is actually *really bad* at hiding anything. But Smalltalk is incredibly good at de-emphasizing the internals of an

object. Why do you care what your microwave looks like inside [except if you are a daughter or son who wants to take my old microwave apart… you know who you are!]? It is doing what you want, so get onto better things. This is the Smalltalk way, and it is incredibly powerful. More than thirty years later it is somewhat mainstream. Which I guess is a classic "Better late than never".

Koi • point three

I said my only resources to save my Koi were my particular skills and the extra forty hours I saved from not being in eighty-hour-a-week mode. But this is clearly not true. I had one other critical resource and it helped me save my Koi. It was friends.

By friends, I don't mean tennis buddies, or some Super Bowl group. I mean coworkers who liked and respected me enough to mention my name when they thought something would match my skills. I can't be sure I know why people care about me, but I do my best to care about my coworkers. I don't do that well with pencil pushers, but with everyone who truly rolls up their sleeves and gets things done, I do my gosh-darned best to treat them with all the respect they deserve. Which is a lot. A lot of respect unless they are clearly not competent or actually antagonistic to the goals of the company.

So a friend from FooMojo was nice enough to introduce me to the CTO of Epocrates. FooMojo was a Rails shop for the web site: Ruby was the language and Rails is a set of technologies to build web sites in Ruby. Epocrates was building a mobile Electronic Medical Record application also in Rails. But they had very little experience in building these kinds of things: historically they built mobile drug reference guides. So this was a big project with lots of unknowns. Any my friend nicely introduced me to the CTO a few months earlier. Turns out the CTO lived only a couple blocks from me, which is one of many great benefits to being in Palo Alto. And through his kindness and my ability to help Epocrates, my friend saved my Koi and me from imminent homelessness.

Homes: Motor • point two

There are three primary classes of RVs used for camping, and they have very simple names: A, B, and C. Of these, only Class-As are commonly motor homes, with all the required elements to be a "house, most mobile". Class Bs are based on converted vans, and Class Cs are converted trucks. Getting both a bathroom and a kitchen into this small a space is very difficult. There are also RVs called travel trailers and fifth-wheels which can have *a lot* of space, but given they need a truck to pull them, they don't pass the "most mobile" requirement, however spacious they are.

To get a true house, most mobile, you need to start with something a bit bigger. You need to be thinking "bus". Big bus. I can hear you thinking: "Normal people don't own busses!" My daughters started shaking their heads a lot when I started seriously discussing motor homes. We would drive down the freeway and I would point at a giant Google Bus, and simply say "About that big". And they would shake their heads some more.

Why do I need a bus-based motor home? Because of a simple constraint: I need two bathrooms. Or at least two toilets, so 1.5 bathrooms. This constraint is to protect the sanity of my Koi and me. Our current house in Palo Alto has only two bathrooms, and my smaller Koi appear to need a lot of time in those bathrooms. So we already have bathroom issues. These issues are big enough to cause family strife and even cause some of us to seek accommodations elsewhere. Going on an RV-based camping trip and not having two bathrooms seemed a recipe for a very bad time. And I would rather not go than go and have a very bad time.

Seven • point two

Startups go through various different growth phases, and the CEO is the person at the helm. Because of the diversity of the phases, being a good CEO through all of them is pretty much impossible. Yes, the big name companies like Apple and Amazon, they had one good CEO through all their successful years, but picking companies of that stature is like putting yourself in with the demigods of any

religion. If or when it turns out you are not a demigod, things are not going to go well.

The first stage of a startup is trying to get enough customer traction that investors can figure out whether you have a viable product and how much that product may be worth. If you build a product but don't sell it, you have not finished the first stage. Even if people put money in because they love you and your product, if this is not based on your actual sales, these people are "angels" and are helping out a company in its first stage. For investment, this is commonly called the "Seed" stage, for your company is a seed that has yet to sprout anything a customer might want.

FooMojo's CEO was clearly very good at the first stage of companies. He had heavy-hitting angels helping him in his seed stage, and when I joined FooMojo they had just landed a significant investment by SoftBank Japan. Approximately ten million dollars. This investment was based on some amazing Facebook growth curves for a flash-based game called FooPets. FooPets were photorealistic virtual pets, which you could play with, feed, dress, and ultimately breed.

When I started working for FooMojo, I was given a ping-pong table. I was on a trial run of my talents to show the CEO I knew how to make software scale in production, and to produce scalability numbers for the software and server infrastructure. FooMojo's growth curves were going very vertical, and the current physical servers could not handle the continual increase in load. Ideally we could simply add more servers and it would handle the additional load of work. Unfortunately, there are commonly bottlenecks and other issues, so we need to make sure FooMojos software don't have any bottlenecks and to find out what its true numbers are.

As an execution specialist, I am thoroughly happy solving a single problem at a time. And this was a big problem. For a week, I ran benchmarks of different (larger) server configurations. It finished with a collection of fixes to the software and reports on how many machines would be required to handle what levels of usage. It also included how we could turn machines on and off easily, ebbing and

flowing with traffic throughout the day. It was not until the end of the week that I was formally hired and given a mug. And a desk.

Community: Tennis

The Mitchell Park tennis community is amongst the most inclusive I have ever run into. It is basically hard *not* to be a part of it if you visit the courts any time before noon. I ultimately became part of the *welcome group* of the community, about nine months after they welcomed me.

Part of the benefit of the park itself is its layout. The tennis backboards are right next to the main four courts. So people can see that you are there hitting against the backboard, and then gauge how good you are by how you are hitting. The gauge isn't to exclude you, it is to match you. Like a dating site.

Mitchell park tennis is ethnically diverse, within the bounds of the ethnicities in Palo Alto that play tennis.

[[TBD]]

Salary: Exposure

So it is apparent why companies have a disincentive to expose salaries: they may be paying people arbitrarily or unfairly, and that would cause employees to be unsatisfied and either ask for a salary adjustment or even cause them to quit. But is there an incentive on the employee part to "keep quiet" about their salary?

I think clearly culturally there is: people who get paid "too much" may not want others to know, and people who get paid "too little" may similarly not want others to know that either. Basically people are embarrassed about themselves. And when I say people, I mean *men*. Men primarily define the rules of the work force. Men have been running the working world for quite some time, and although women are now impacting it, there is little chance that they have dramatically changed the rules. Yet.

So men don't want other men to see their salary. Most men don't want direct exposure of "what I am worth" for the entire world to see. They want to hide it. Men try to hide everything they can be evaluated on, and then deny the rest really matters.

I think women think differently. Women are already heavily evaluated on very exposed traits. You can see their beautiful faces and beautiful bodies, and decide "wow" or "no". I was getting coffee at Zoom Caffe[53] and one of the patrons was a "Bikini-class Bodybuilder". She had recently started to compete, and remarked that it was a little difficult to have spectators closely staring at her body. At first. But she got used to it. Even draped with loose fitting clothes, it was clear she had an amazingly beautiful body. She worked on it, and she earned it. That day she was going to splurge on a Soy Latte. For the next few weeks leading to the next competition, it was only espresso for her.

After my tenth startup, I was quite fat. The stress and time commitment of startups had caused me to "let it go" in ways that seriously affected my waistline and health. Fortunately one of my daughters asked me to teach her how to play tennis. I had enough time, and enough commitment that her simple request caused me to lose 40 pounds of fat, and gain 10 pounds of muscle. I am no longer fat.

When I went to buy a suit, so I could testify in court or blend in with my East Coast counterparts, I inquired about made-to-measure suits. MTMs cost about 20% more if the same material. You can also get some materials for MTMs that you can't get off the rack. I picked one beautiful material, and it priced out at $33K! I decided to not wear a car. And I also decided not to go the MTM route. I wear a 40R, and off the rack a 40R fit me perfectly. Or really, I fit a 40R perfectly. I was not fat or skinny. Through efforts during the prior year, I was "built". So if we got the shoulders right, and hemmed the pants, everything else pretty much fell into place.

---

[53] A very interesting variation of a food truck that just does coffee drinks

When talking to the tailors and sales people for my suit, they remarked how good I looked in the suit with minimal alterations, and remarked about other customers who would *complain* that the tailor was doing a bad job of making them look good in their suits. They paid several thousand dollars for a suit, and expected it would look good on them. But their waste was in the 40s or 50s. The tailor had no hope. The men were exposed because you just cannot hide certain things.

So maybe we men should stop trying to hide all manner of things and own up to who we really are. And then be better than that.

Seven • point three

After becoming the actual VP Engineering for FooMojo, I oversaw a relatively junior team that had been directly run by the CEO. The CEO thought of himself as a programmer in spite of no training and insignificant experience. One of the fallacies of modern software programming is that people feel it is incredibly important. And everyone has a computer with free programming software on it. So if you just learn to use the tools, you are now a programmer.

Maybe this is the problem with many professions, but it seems especially problematic with software. This is likely because a computer can not critique what you ask it to do. A general contractor can scoff an architect or bridge engineer that draws something stupid. But a computer will happily comply with whatever you tell it to do. And if this appears to "work" you are now a programmer.

So the CEO was the lead programmer during stage one, but we are now in stage two. There are a couple dozen people with most of them being in the art group. The art group is primarily trying to create, animate, and render (virtually film) photorealistic dogs and cats and environments. The CEO also was the lead of the art team in stage one. Stage one had three people answering to the CEO. Stage two has two dozen. That is a lot more people, and a lot more activity, and effectively the CEO "snapped".

Commitment: Failer

[[TBD]]

A professional failer is someone who… it is Tris, with a bit of Amity and Candor thrown in.

Food: Chinatown

Initially our primary Chinese destination was downtown Chinatown. This was a "straight shot" down the 110 raceway into an exit on the left. I think picking cars and destination took longer than the drive. My roommate at Caltech is Chinese, as is Rebecca. Rebecca has big, beautiful, eyes. She also has big eyes for food. So our table always ordered a lot of food. Very good food. Another advantage of Chinese food is that leftovers are better and easier to deal with than for most other foods. But I don't actually recall ever having leftovers.

We later shifted to Monterey Park, which had a different kind of Chinese food. It was generally more authentic food because the ethnic immigration was more recent. The drive was very boring.

Seven • point four

"CEOs don't just 'snap'! They are well-trained serial entrepreneurs that are given custody of millions of dollars." I admit, before FooMojo, I had never seen anything like this. But a company with a perfectly reasonable (if silly) product vision, an amazing growth story, great artists, and reasonable technology went completely bonkers.

We had the Apple Marketing splash page showing two of our iPhone games during the Christmas season. These games made a lot of money. And both were canceled by February. We had a great presence on Facebook with nice growth curves. And we were off Facebook in time for Christmas, losing hundreds of thousands of users. We had a fun game for Valentine's day called Heart Park, and it was killed shortly thereafter. And a final command that fortunately

never went "live", is that he wanted the pets to die so kids could experience loss (and have to buy new pets).

It was a wild and crazy ride. I offered to help with the broader team and company management, but this was rejected, and I simply left shortly after the Heart Park release. We had a great team at FooMojo, but one person can ruin the bunch.

Fini Seven

Family: Eastern

To be part of an Eastern family, you must obey the rules of eastern families. These rules include a very simple "show up" rule. If someone is getting married, you show up. If someone dies, you show up. People may not know your name, or speak your language, but if you continue to show up, people will take notice of that, and will eventually start expecting you to show up more no matter how strange you look. This is kind of like "Wedding Crashers" but somehow flipped in its universe.

Next you must do *whatever you can do* for other family members. If someone wants to visit Palo Alto, and you live in Palo Alto, then you should offer them room,.board, tourism, and even the "how to get a job here" package. You may have met the person, or they could be a distant third cousin twice removed. The offer is the same. These things are very easy to offer if you view the clan as just a *little larger* than your atomic family: you would certainly do any of these things trivially for you son or daughter, right?

Finally, when you become an elder in an eastern family, you should graciously pay for all meals and produce great quantities of large value "hongbao" (red pockets). Red pockets are envelopes, and in them is *money*. Hongbao are the primary mechanism to enable elders to transfer wealth to non-atomic youngsters in the extended family. I believe I have the order right, and *doing* is more meaningful than *financing*, but I am not sure. Large amounts of money move via Hongbao, and having a geographically near Aunt (#6) and Uncle has prevented me from being put into the true elder position and bearing

the full weight of the intra-family financing. But Rebecca and I are ready whenever we are promoted: however Western I am on the outside, I am a Shen on the inside. I have lots of new hundred-dollar bills, which could easily be placed inside fancy red envelopes. I love this family.

Right: Team

Assembling the right team for a startup is very difficult. First, you don't have a great value proposition to team members. You are offering longer hours for less pay in exchange for a small chance of valuable stock. And in exchange for being able to create something, almost from scratch. This pitch tends to attract people that are somewhat delusional about (a) the chance for success and (b) their abilities to create something from scratch. Very few people do startup-after-startup, so very few people really know how to launch a startup reliably.

So you may not get quite right people, but some are willing to take a chance on your idea. Next the team has to be balanced and organized properly. Startups are not a tea party. They are not a Quaker meeting. They are not a democracy. They are a dictatorship: one person is the leader, and the rest start filling in the details of execution. Why? Because *there is no time* for anything but a dictatorship. Startups are like a military operation: you need to get it done with as few casualties as possible. The longer you are in operation as a startup, the more casualties you will have.

Under the dictator should be people that the dictator trusts to execute the high level needs of the company. A fan-out of three is probably ideal, but slightly more or less is fine depending on what the roles are. In some companies I have been in, it has been an "Outside-Inside-Finance" triplet with the CEO being "Outside", a COO being "Inside", and the CFO being "Finance and Accounting". The CEO could be so busy raising money or doing specialty customer interaction that they need a head of Sales/Marketing to be at the table as a second "Outside" representative.

Note that I am using the "puffy" titles mostly because they work well from the top-down. In a startup, things are so small that all titles are ridiculous except in how they reflect your relationship to the dictator. A VP Engineering reports to the COO which reports to the CEO. The VP Engineering could have a team the size of the VP Engineering (i.e. one) and the title still makes some sense working from top down. From bottom up, the person is simply an "engineer" and not even a manager.

So as you work out the company, you add as few layers as possible and keep each layer as small as possible. You are trying to minimize head count. For both cost and interaction overhead. If four people can get in a room and do everything, than don't add ten more people. Think "squad" until "squad" doesn't work for some objectively obvious reason. An example is 3-D art as is common in games. If you don't have a lot of it, one multi-talented person can handle it. But as the load on the art team increases, it will either have to grow, outsource some of the work, or push back and say "this will be expensive, can we do this instead?"

Wrong: Leader

The right team for a startup includes a dictator at the helm. That may sound scary, but it is better for the startup's chance of success than any other model I have seen. The dictator could be benevolent and highly competent. Or highly competent and a real terror. Either of these are good for the startup, if not great for the team. You can't be competent and a terror at the same time unless you are pretty good at balancing that terror with something else (e.g. Steve Jobs' praise).

But if you have a dictator at the helm, your company is hopeless if they are incompetent. Incompetency is the inability to see how good or bad you are at something. A competent dictator who is bad at fund-raising, hooks up with someone who is good at fund-raising. And the problem is at least partially solved. A competent dictator who is bad with people, gets a right-hand who is great with people and again, the problem is at least partially solved. Really, the only thing the dictator *has* to be good at is determining *what* they are not

good at. And then filling in that hole. It might cost equity, money, or even the reigns to the company, but a good founder of a startup is willing to give any and all of that away in exchange for the startup (his or her baby) to survive.

Kindness: Bread

After taking the red pill, I started doing things my family considered quite insane, but I can no longer identify as such. Amongst the simplest of these was buying and giving away bread.

This was not any old bread, but was some amazing bread sold by a great restaurant and baker named Manresa. Our family has been going to the Mountain View farmers market for the last two decades. [[TBD]]

EIGHT

I left FooMojo out of self-preservation. A CEO that kills successful products, interferes with his leads abilities to do their job, and is not interested in getting any kind of help from anyone… that is the captain of a ship *guaranteed* to go under really soon. So I fled rapidly, and before I had anything else set up.

Fortunately, my skills in mobile, games, and servers were highly valued in Silicon Valley. A few job posting responses, and I was offered a salary and 10% of a company that wanted a mobile, fun, health and wellness platform. That company was Vive.

The salary was a bit quirky: they wanted me to accept a third off for the first (pretty much full) month. That should have been a red flag, but I didn't see it. Just seemed quirky, but not a big deal. Vive had a prototype in Flash with a Microsoft backend[54]. Also a bit quirky because Flash was not mobile capable at the time, and Microsoft technology is not commonly used for backends, at least not commonly in startups in Silicon Valley. So my goals as I understood them were (a) to move to a reasonable stack[55] for mobility and scalability, (b) build out the real functionality they wanted[56], and (c) make it as much fun as if it were a game.

I believe I totally conquered two of those goals, but the third was "an incorrect understanding" on my part. I was just hired away from a gaming company, to make a product fun, but no one really wanted it to be fun at all. Or at least no one could decide *what* they wanted it to be at all. I was in a tea-party reminiscent of Alice in Wonderland.

---

[54] The "backend" is the part of an application that is running on servers separate from the device you are interacting with. If you have a smart phone, it can have applications on it, but to safely save data and do interesting inter-personal capabilities requires a 'backend' that all the phones are talking to

[55] Set of technologies

[56] The prototype was pretty barren

Failer: Tennis

Tennis is the ultimate Failer sport. It isn't just a failer sport in practice. You could say golf or archery is similar if you just don't count missed shots. But tennis is very different: it supports failing all the way to Wimbledon final matches. It embraces failing so you can see how amazing success can be.

The number of different ways tennis gives second chances is amazing. First, you get two serves. Why? Well obviously in case you fail your first serve. Even better, this encourages you to produce a more awesome first serve, because you have a second chance. Even if you use exactly the same awesome serve twice, as long as you get near 80% with your serve, you have excellent odds of success. You should only double fault four times every hundred serves.

Second, you must win or lose each game by two points. Lose one, win one, and you are back where you started. So go for the win if you can, because at worse you are at a disadvantage. And you might just get an advantage.

Third, you must win or lose each set by two games. Additionally you usually can lose one or two sets and still win the match. It may be harder to win at a disadvantage, but it is definitely possible.

Finally, every shot you lose does not penalize your position. You didn't hit a ball into the rough. You didn't lose position on the field. Miss a shot, and the whole thing starts over, exactly where you started.

Maybe some other sport is similar, but Tennis seems to totally embrace this ability to fail, so great athletes can give it there all.

Koi • point four

To closure the story, I worked part time for Epocrates while continuing to work for the "shorting" startup. The contracting paid just enough to prevent the aquarium from draining, and I had plenty

of time to keep the startup chugging along. They did ask less of me during this period, so having to do an 80-hour week for them while getting very little cash was fortunately not on the table. Apparently shorting your employees makes you feel slightly guilty.

A couple months in and a pair of Angel investors start being interested in the "shorting" startup. I was hopeful: maybe I would be paid my back pay if they put in some more money. But alas, the timeline of these angels does not look to be any time soon. And the "shorting" startup cuts my salary to one quarter, apparently motivated by an email of mine with the highly defensive words "You can pay me half or nothing, but I can't get this done any sooner". This was while I was working about 40 hours a week for them. So I get paid about two gallons a month for a few more months until finally they formally terminate me. I never received any final paycheck or unused vacation reimbursement… just a letter telling me how many worthless shares I had in their worthless company. I join the next startup almost immediately.

Employees: Labor Commissioner

I know the facts at the end of the Koi story in vivid detail because of a very funny story. Several years after working for the startup in Koi, I get an email from the angel investors. They ultimately did invest in the startup, and although the last three years did not go great, they want to give the company another go with a new CEO. To do that, all the existing creditors and investors (including people with worthless common, like me) need to sign a contract stating that creditors get nothing (I guess) and investors get one hundredth of what they have now. So if I owned 2% of the worthless company, I would now own 0.02% of the worthless company.

Legally, for a contract to be valid it must have mutual consideration: both parties must benefit from the contract. Any one-way contract is not enforceable. A detrimental contract (one party is hurt in exchange for another's benefit) is not enforceable. And forcing someone to take less in consideration after they fulfill their side of the contract is not enforceable.

So I see the terms being offered me in the contract: less of something worthless in exchange for nothing, and I recognize this as being "insane". So I ignore it, and hope the angels will go away. I am currently doing well at filling the aquarium, so I don't want to be distracted by bad memories. A month later I get another mass email. Again I ignore it. Another three mass emails come in March with some 40 people on the distribution, then 35, and then 30. So clearly a number of people were signing up to these insane contracts. Or maybe it somehow made more sense in their particular cases.

But then the dreaded day comes: an email to me specifically. "We have not received your signed document… Can you please execute it today or tomorrow?" I respond that I could not see what was in it for me, and that I had lost well over $60K due to salary non-payment. The first response from the angels' is "everyone lost a lot of money".

This is why I want anyone reading this book to take at least one thing about startups to heart. You *want* to be an employee. Employees are special. They are *protected.*

Eight • point two

Vive floated through a large number of offices during the time I was with the company. I am not sure which of these offices cost rent and which were donated to the owners. A startup working out of donated office space saves a lot of money, and although houses are not ideal locations, they can be reasonable if they work out for the employees. Vive's "main" office during my time with them was inside an investment branch of Ask.com. It was a nice building along California Avenue in Palo Alto. I could have walked or biked to the office but because I carried a pretty heavy computer bag, I drove a few blocks to convenient parking and walked the rest.

In the first few months I moved the Vive architecture off the Microsoft technology and onto a normal Linux and Java based technology stack. The GUI was in a product called YUI by Yahoo (Yahoo User Interface) and was among the technologies trying to do web clients that work well on both desktop and mobile devices.

Unfortunately this happened to be a period where Yahoo started shrinking, so the technology did not really keep up well compared to other ones. And Yahoo was not really very good with mobile devices at this time either. In the end, YUI worked but was not great, especially after coming from Flash and native iPhone user interfaces.

Food: Chopsticks

The lore around chopsticks is that they were invented to avoid having men stab each other. Knives in the kitchen. Blunt chopsticks in the eating hall. Although movies sometimes show otherwise, it is very hard to kill someone with a chopstick. So large groups of drunken men could safely eat, drink, and try to kill each other without any actual fatalities.

Presumably to people born in China, Korea, and similar countries, chopsticks are the most natural thing in the universe. You just put two sticks into your hand and pick things (even peanuts) up with them.

As a biological fork eater, I have to say eating with chopsticks was amongst the most bizarrely challenging obstacles I have ever overcome. But it was also the perfect challenge. I was hungry. There was food in front of me. I could see my Chinese friends eating the food in front of them. So…

Within about a year, I was clearly proficient. And within say four years of part-time chopstick usage, I could use them like a native. There are a total of three ways to use a pair of chopsticks: like a native (only one stick moves), like a novice (both sticks move), and like a failure (ask for fork). Caltech graduates are never a failure, but only some of us biological-fork-users progressed to being native chopstick users.

Chakras: Unblocking

My family lives in Palo Alto, which is renowned in the area for having the best school system. The resources of the schools are very

good, and our children went to elementary school there. But the mandatory curriculum of California (and maybe the US) makes it so students have very little freedom to explore their interest. And we are also a feminine household, and are very worried about girls being treated poorly in school. As of middle school, both of my daughters are no longer in our wonderful Palo Alto public schools. They go to Girls Middle School and Nueva High School. This is very expensive, but we are already spending more than $60K a year on just the house itself. So with the flood of money going out, a few more streams are not going to kill me any faster.

I believe the money is provably well spent. Not everyone can afford it, and our family is trying to help the public schools too. Rebecca works for Palo Alto Partner's in Education (PIE), which raises additional funding for special programs in Palo Alto schools. But the kids progressing through GMS and Nueva have much fewer blocked chakras than most kids I have encountered from other schools. So we are spending money to unblock our daughters and our daughters' classmates chakras. To make the next generation *better* than we are.

I was visiting Nueva as a new parent, and a girl was asking about the Nueva Quest program. The Quest program allows kids to explore an interest for a year or two, and it can basically be an interest in almost anything. One girl learned to dance aerial silks. A boy built a robotic chessboard. Another boy is learning how to write and produce a movie. And another girl had great interest in ancient maps, and learned how to make them. The students' quests are supposed to have a mentor. For example, the ancient maps quest student had an Oxford Professor helping her. So returning to the girl above, she was asking the teacher overseeing the program how students find their mentors. The answer was "Either on their own, or alumni and parents and faculty can help". The next question was "What about in medicine, like a doctor?" The answer was, yes that is easy, "The only quest we are having problems finding a mentor for is video game design."

I get directions to the student's booth and quickly wander over. He is busy showing his game to other students, so I keep it very

short. I speak to him and write on a piece of paper: "Google Rumble Games. My name is Mark Fussell. My email address is this…". Basically the same pitch I gave to S. The student had never met me before, and was several years younger than S.

Thirty-six hours later, I get an email. I am now a mentor, to the Nueva student 'N'.

N has unblocked chakras, or at least many more unblocked than S.

Eight • point three

After solving the mobile problem and moving the backend to a reasonable production architecture, we were ready to go live. Initially the product just sent reminders and tip-of-the-day messages to people, and let people journal their daily activities. This was not compelling and did not produce great customer interaction. We had a running product that was not being used.

The core product questions for any startup are "Who are our customers?" and "What do they want?". Vive was in the wellness space and I was hired to help make wellness fun. So I came up with lots of "games" that involved actual physical activity. Games like having to physically run around to get ahead of your competitors race (using a pedometer like a Fitbit), or doing a capture-the-flag virtual race whoever gets to the location of a flag first wins it (using GPS like Shadow Cities). And various ideas that seemed like they would be fun to someone about thirty five years old or older.

Our primary customers were employers trying to reduce health costs by getting their employees in better shape. Targeting people older than thirty five seemed reasonable, because that is the time period where people commonly stop doing sports and become more sedentary. So our users were older workers and our customers were there companies. We were trying to make both of them happy as quickly as possible.

Startups: Tea Parties

I have never worked for a startup that was officially run by a woman. That would actually be very interesting. The best female bosses I have had, including my mother[57], have managed to make sure the team knew where we were supposed to head, to clear away any obstacles for us, and to make us all feel like we were cared about. That is very good management, in my opinion. Some of the managers were a little more project management oriented, and status updates mattered a lot to them. Some were a little less connected with the team. But in general I have had excellent female managers over the last thirty years.

The closest I had to a startup run by women, was a startup run by a man and a woman where the man "managed like a woman". And by that, I mean it to match the expression "throw like a girl". In reality, girls throw really well. I threw my arm out trying to pitch softball… and my daughter now pitches softball… so to me "throwing like my daughter" is clearly a complement. And despite the fact that women manage really well, there are stereotypes about how they might do it ineffectively. This particular startup somehow decided to follow one of those stereotypes. This startup was run by tea party.

We would all get together several times a week, sit around a table, and bring up one or more topics. Tea was not officially served, but certain people would definitely be eating. Others would be lunging… apparently good exercise and socially acceptable at the tea party. Topics would come and go, and by the end of the meeting we would have covered absolutely everything on the agenda. But absolutely nothing had been decided.

There are great benefits to tea parties. By deciding nothing each time, you could have many more tea parties and not run out of topics. If you actually had a normal meeting, the number of topics would dwindle as the company truly executed upon an actual strategy. There were times we had real meetings at this startup, and

---

[57] I worked for her nonprofit when I was young, as a programmer and general computer-person

for a couple months I was hopeful. But even actual forward progress can be thwarted by "maybe we need to rethink this", and another series of tea parties. Tea parties about user interfaces[58] are my favorite.

Boxes: Mavvi • point two

On the week before my family's Yosemite trip, the project managers for Mavvi were estimating and scheduling what should be done in the next "iteration". Mavvi uses a two-week period starting on a Thursday and ending on a Wednesday to organize and synchronize work. Each of these periods is called "an iteration", and this slicing of time is a common structure in several agile methodologies. For Mavvi, there are endless meetings at the start and end of each iteration, talking about what to do next and what was done previously. All these meeting cause each iteration have a lot of overhead, and it really makes them not agile at all despite the "attempt".

The Yosemite trip occurred during iteration 253. As mentioned above, I was achieving about 25 to 50 points per iteration. But I was going away. And I was not expecting to show up again until very late in iteration 253. So I told people to not include "my capacity" in the estimates and schedules. I would pick a few things up when I got back, but there was no reason to estimate it… just queue up a "small amount" of work for me without committing to it getting done with senior management. I would get done what I could, all of which would be 'bonus'.

Unfortunately, project management did not follow my suggestion. My 25-50 points of development capacity was included in iteration 253. And various people, who historically accomplish less than 3 points per iteration, were given my tasks. Somehow miraculously they would suddenly quadruple their productivity.

[58] The interface between the product and the user, which includes what kinds of 'widgets' (menus, check boxes, etc.) to use and especially, painfully, includes a whole bunch of stylistic choices commonly made by people with no knowledge of either style or effectiveness

The Yosemite trip was very nice, and I did not read my email or look at the state of the world while there. I was with my family, and we did many fun outings together. I love Yosemite, and this was a perfect time of year to go there.

I returned to Mavvi less than a week before iteration 253 ends. There are many tasks of mine that were given to various other people. Absolutely *none* of them had even been started. Apparently the various other people had various other things to do, so they couldn't even start on my 25-50 points of work. At this point, I could just let it go and watch the crash and burn of iteration 253. There would be 254 right after it. Let everyone get badly burned once, and learn from their mistake. But I am a startup kind of guy, and if I see something needs to be done, I simply do it.

Over several days, which include the entire weekend, I "pick up" and knock off this backlog of tasks assigned to various other people. I can take ownership of them, and move them into "Please Verify" with the permissions I have in JIRA. I can also take ownership of other tasks that have aspects of what I need to get done now. But I can't move these into '253'. And I can't change things from 'Please Verify' to 'Done'. I don't have the proper permissions to do these minor project management tasks. I need someone else to do it for me.

During the weekend, I make these requests "Please move what I am currently working on into iteration 253.", "Please verify that what I have finished is actually working as expected.", and so on. Nothing happens. On Monday I request it again. Nothing.

On Tuesday, the "architect" starts chiming in that although what I have done works, it isn't what he wants. He wants my code to *not work*. To pretend it works by 'mocking' out the behavior. Then after I pretend it works, I can go back and make it *work* again.

Further, because I am doing things I shouldn't be doing yet, these things should not be moved into 253. Reality does not trump the plan. Must follow the plan. Yes, I have actually *finished* all these things, so the plan is now nonsensical. But a nonsensical plan is

better than a surprisingly good reality.

Although my customer is happy, and all of product management is happy, the "architect" gets to derail me. After I sacrificed a whole weekend with my family trying to help Mavvi get C3 out the door.

Mavvi does postmortems: reviewing what went well and what they could improve. I do not attend the postmortem for 253, but I do tell them what they could do better by email: "Be appreciative and respectful of others". Those are not my exact words, but they are close.

By Friday we all agree to end Experiment Three. C3 was basically done when I stopped working on it. I am not sure if it has gone live in the many months that have passed. I think not.

Eight • point four

Unfortunately, Vive didn't seem to be able to make any decisions at all. People would come up with partially developed ideas, and then they would be shelved. I would provide a working prototype of something and it would be looked at but never "approved". Instead I kept getting requests to move buttons around or change the color of something or another. This was trivial work, and took me almost no time for each request. But then request after request would come through.

About the time of trivial requests came two other major events for Vive. First, we moved into a single room office about six feet by ten feet. At the time there were as many as six of us, so we could barely fit into this office space standing, and certainly could not work within it. This was clearly a sign of money running out. The second sign was my paycheck suddenly being halved. This and the ongoing events are written up within a different thread.

At this point, I am clearly not fired because *everything* was running on my credit card and I was the only technical person in the company. I was still working more than forty hours a week for Vive to try to get it to succeed. But I had very little money in the bank

due to the sequences of failed startups. And I needed cash... fast...

Family: Western

My western family that lives to the east seemed very normal to me as a child, but now seems almost bizarre. As a child, we would get together for Christmas, Thanksgiving, and maybe Easter, and the kids would play together and eat (or not) candied yams together at the kids dining table. The adults would all eat at the main dining table. Everything whirled around my mother's parent's house, which was just a few minutes away from ours.

But these events were happenstance and not sincere. The family did not grow from strong roots, but from the last pretenses of being related before deciding to go separate ways. Tumbleweeds. Although we invited everyone to Rebecca and my wedding ceremony in California and a reception Philadelphia, few came to see us be wedded [and be tortured with great wine and great food], and some didn't even wander a couple cities away to join the reception. And when others became married, we were commonly not invited. In one case, we did a special trip to Maine for a wedding anniversary, and our newborn daughter Maya was so endearing it somehow made us a pariah in the state.

So we no longer visit family in Maine, but still have good friends in Portland. If 'E' visited us in Palo Alto, he would immediately become part of our atomic family, and the last time we visited Boston, 'E' bussed down for a day walking the city. Rebecca and I love Boston.

Whether the western family will transform, I do not know. I cannot personally take responsibility for it, but if it wants to change, I certainly have a model for what a true family is like. A true family has rules, and commitments. All based out of love.

Right: Partner

Finding the right partner depends a huge amount on what you and

your partner are trying to do together and the duration of that partnership commitment. The longer and larger the task, the less important "picking" the right partner is compared to becoming good partners. The commitment to grow together trumps any starting picking advantage. This is the positive side of arranged marriages: if you can't pick your partner, your only option is to commit to loving and growing with the one picked for you. "Love the one you're with". Many couples with the freedom to choose and re-choose their partners separate due to irreconcilable differences, possibly a euphemism for "Too hard, not really that committed".

For startups, on the other hand, you have to pick well because you only have months or a few years to succeed. You are not looking for partners who you easily get along with. You are looking for opposites (complements) that you can communicate with. Although being the CEO/President will always be lonely, you want your earliest partners to be as close to peers of a different ilk as you can find. Steve Jobs and Steve Wozniak appear to have been great partners with very different interests and abilities, and with the capacity to get along together despite their differences. Unfortunately, I never encountered that kind of pairing nor could I make it happen in my own startup. Likely the closest to it was little Evant (three). The team was diverse enough in talents, but there were too many members of the leadership group. One of my last startups had a good dynamic between me and the business and product manager, but another person held the reins to the venture as a whole and would break our rhythms just when we got into a good stride.

For life partners I have had some amazing luck and success based on seriously amounts of commitment and effort. But over a total of ten startups, either the partnership didn't happen or we ran out of time before it could really shine.

Wrong: Ethic

It is unclear to me whether businesses have to be ethical. There is a lot of evidence to me over decades of work that businesses simply try to look ethical and then do whatever they can to succeed. I am

not sure whether this is taught in MBA programs, a secret society, or just the inner circles of the company know they are not going to be ethical (even law-abiding) and it gets transferred to the chosen apprentice.

A lot of employees don't seem to care. They work nine to five and head home. They don't notice when someone gets "let go" and replaced by a woman thirty years younger. Or they notice and simply go "hmm", and carry on with life.

Unfortunately, I can not turn a blind eye to these things and it is increasing my frustration working with certain companies. I want businesses to succeed but to have good morals to both their goals with their customers and their goals with their team. Less than half the startups I have worked for and with have good morals to both.

Kindness: Fairness

Caltech had a simple honor code "Don't take unfair advantage of anyone". I am not sure all Techers believed in this code, but I know it resonated with me. I will happily crush you on the tennis court, because I have earned that right. Or maybe you will crush me because you actually *are* Federer, and have talents and experience beyond my own. I prefer games like Go where you can handicap the better player and have a very even game in spite of skill differences. But whether handicapped or not, these are all fair.

Unfair is where you are taking advantage of someone else's unfortunate position relative to you. If you can not afford a tennis racket, and instead play with a broom, I will not play with you. That would be unfair and just simply bizarre. I will give you one of my rackets to make things fair, and from there we can have a good day. You can keep the racket, because clearly you need one.

Caltech's simple honor code of fairness became solidified in my head when I read a much longer treatise on the topic. Rawls "Theory of Justice" had a simple way of determining fairness, which I described earlier. You have multiple roles, you don't know which you are in, now describe what is fair. And maybe we roll some dice

to see where you land today. And another roll tomorrow. And so on.

Playing this kind of game would make you very aware of what seemed fair on either side. It wouldn't just make us sympathetic, we would be truly empathetic. And we would always want the alternatives to be as fair as possible from each of their perspectives. Complete knowledge of what the possibilities were, and complete ignorance of which possibility we were going to get.

This concept of true fairness would get rid of a lot of social problems and inequalities.

NINE

While Vive was shorting me, I was looking for both consulting work and a replacement job that paid a bit better than the shorted ½ or ¼ of an already 'discounted' salary. My standard process for finding jobs 'cold' is relatively simple: I review my primary sources for jobs (LinkedIn and Craigslist), see if the job and company sound interesting, review all the materials possible online about the company, and then craft a cover letter specific to that company. I organize these searches around quarters: in 2010Q2 I did this for a position posted by Eveo, a full-service pharmaceutical advertising company. I believe it was something like CTO or Director of IT, and I passed the screens well enough to interview with the CEO of Eveo.

The company was in the northeast corner of San Francisco, and although I found the building interesting, curving that far around the Embarcadero took a long time. This did not bode well for me working there, since I care about my time a lot. But I met with the CEO and had a pleasant discussion about who I was, what I could do, and what they were looking for. I was also pleasantly surprised to find out that they were going to move into a more normal part of San Francisco, a few minutes from the train and the 280 landing points. Everything seemed normal, but then he says "You are perfect!" But he wasn't referring to the position we were discussing, it was clearly something else. And he wouldn't tell me what it was. Not with an NDA[59]. Not at all. I was perfect… for something.

A couple months pass (Vive was paying me only ¼ my salary by this time), and I get an email from the CEO. Could I come in, this time to the new office? I say "sure". This commute was much easier: they were in what used to be the Razorfish offices and it was barely not-under the Oakland Bay Bridge. This better location saved

---

[59] Non-disclosure agreement. An agreement that in exchange for being given information you promise to not disclose it to others. These are very common in the startup world where most CEOs think their idea is so wonderfully original and powerful that simply disclosing it to another entrepreneur will instantly create competition or even victory in them

at least half an hour of commute time. The office space was quite large and open, but not everyone had moved in yet. And I think they were expecting to grow. We went into a very open conference room: today I would find out what the CEO had in mind. I think I signed an NDA, and with that joined the project/startup of PeerCase.

Tennis: Punting

I started playing tennis after 29 years because Katrina asked to play. We had to buy new rackets, and some tennis balls. Tennis rackets have changed size since when I was young (possibly to continue to embrace failure), and although the size change brought forth some silly rackets, modern rackets are quite fun to play with. And modern high-speed photography has made it possible to see how the professionals play. I decided that my game when I was young, and my mentality now, made Federer the perfect person to copy. I wanted a one-handed powerful forehand, and a one-handed powerful backhand, and a high-percentage but powerful serve. I was willing to work at these things, and spent many hours a week on the backboard, with a ball machine, and playing people better than me.

During the first six months, my forehand and backhand came alone nicely. My volleys did also, but I am innately a touch player, so that wasn't very impressive to me. The one thing that did not come along nicely was my serve.

Sometimes I would mishit the ball badly, and sometimes I tore muscles I didn't know I had. My percentage serving my first serve was very iffy. After six months, I was generally better than most other players I was playing with, but when it came to my serve, I had serious problems. I practiced my serve on my own, and tried to figure out what was going on in matches. I reviewed Federer videos and listened to both solicited and unsolicited advice from others. But there is one thing I never did.

I never 'punted'. I had one serve, and if it failed, it failed. I served it again, and tried to do better. Federer has at least two real serves. The may behave differently, but neither is a punt. He may actually

have many more serves, and like my tennis coach, he can use all of these *impressive* serves as he wants. But club tennis players don't commonly have two serves. They have one serve and a punt. Their second serve is just meant to get the ball in play. Federer doesn't have a punt, so I don't either. I don't want to *practice* something I don't want. I practice what I do want. And accept failure if I fail.

A few players griped to me about my needing to get the ball into play. If everyone griped and I had no one to play with, I would happily accept that. I clearly needed to practice on my own more. But I was good enough that most players accepted my iffy serve in exchange for my other talents.

About nine months in, my iffy serve became no longer as iffy. It became pretty dangerous. Nine months of failing, and I was finally succeeding. I serve at about 90 MPH. Federer is better, but none of the gripers are even close.

I then started learning a second real serve. At first it was very iffy.

Nine • point two

PeerCase is only "mostly" a startup. It had a vision, insane deadlines, a tiny team, and many of the other trappings of a startup. But when I eventually became a W-2, it was with Eveo and not PeerCase. I had a salary but was never made an equity offer at all. A big part of doing startups is the hope that the startup would succeed and you would get a piece of that success. But PeerCase was a startup incubated in Eveo, smothered by it's mother's love, and ultimately the inability to spin PeerCase out from it's mother would be its downfall.

But in late 2010, PeerCase had a very strong and clear vision: enable oncologists to easily share their more serious cancer cases with experts in each of the types of cancers. If you have melanoma, you really need to talk to an expert in *Pennsylvania* who knows the latest treatments. Cancer treatments can change monthly, and each change improves your chances of living longer. Potentially *much*

longer.

PeerCase had the best specifications for it's desired UI[60] and functionality I had ever seen this early in a project. There were some number of wireframes, and also several pixel-perfect graphical treatments. Wireframes are where you show all the elements in a UI, but don't worry about their color and other styling. Usually you do most functional things as wireframes, since it is much easier to iterate on[61] them. They are like sketches.

The pixel-perfect graphical treatments are like paintings: take one or more sketches and paint all the detailed colors, specify exact fonts, and so on. Having pixel-perfect graphical treatments can either be a blessing or a curse. If the pixel-perfect treatments are meant to be inspirational and direction indicating, they are a blessing. You see the styling that people want, and then depending on your UI framework's capabilities either match exactly (say in Adobe Flash), or get reasonably close and keep the inspiration intact (say in HTML5). The alternative is that the pixel-perfect treatments are *requirements.* You must comply with them even if doing so was insanely expensive in software. Software is alive and has to *work.* Paintings are just that: a pretty picture.

Eveo was an advertising agency and made movies. They did not understand software and its restrictions. When the CEO chose an HTML5 approach over Flash (so it could be on the iPad), I had no chance of cost-effectively reproducing the pixel-perfect treatments. To their credit, they did ultimately accept this, but it was initially very difficult to explain.

The thing that made it easiest is that PeerCase also had a very strong and clear vision of its timeline: Go live by ASH. ASH stands for The American Society of Hematology. It has a conference the second week of December, and that year it was to be in Florida. From the point the CEO told me what he wanted to the point of the conference was just weeks. This was going to be very much like Evant, where I am satisfying all of Vive, my family, and PeerCase

---

[60] User Interface

[61] Refine and change

simultaneously. To make this work this time was going to take a bit of blood.

Programming: Bleeding Edge

Bleeding edge refers to technology that is a bit immature and untested, and by using it you are taking a chance that it will cut you. A little bit of blood could be worth the benefits: either greater performance, special new capability, or a productivity boost. Make the wrong choice (basically, trust the wrong team or misunderstand the technology), and your project will bleed to death. So much time and effort will be going into stopping the bleeding, or even having to restart everything, your project will run out of time and money.

To make PeerCase possible in the ridiculously short period before ASH required either using the best possible mainstream technologies, or using some up and coming technologies that promised to do great things. For building capable UIs, Adobe Flash & Flex were amongst the most productive. I knew them well from Velidom, Winster, and FooMojo. Someone skilled with them could whip up UIs in almost no time flat.

But we were targeting IOS devices (specifically iPads) for their gloss and simplicity. So Flash was out. There were a few HTML5 technologies, but only one that was really close to the abilities of a native IOS device: Sencha Touch. Sencha Touch was made by a team with a long history of expertise in Javascript. It had a lot of good things in its core, but also had a fair amount of bugs and peculiar behavior. So I had to fix or avoid those idiosyncrasies to make sure the application looked good and behaved well.

Employees: Labor Commissioner • point two

I like negotiating with people when everyone behaves reasonably. I don't negotiate on very many things: you have a price for your product, I will either buy it or not at that price. I might wait for a sale, but even that is unlikely. I certainly won't say your price is unreasonable and I would like it to just be less. When I was in India

I had my Indian friends and my Indian driver haggle for me, because there it is normal and expected.

But if something has no obvious price, negotiating over what the price should be is totally reasonable to me. A startup wanted to get my signature on a contract, and I wanted to be compensated for unpaid wages. I estimated the number as $60K, but my first generous offer is to include $30K of my consulting services as part of the $60K. This way, I am effectively being paid in the future, so it doesn't look like I was given different and special treatment compared to other creditors.

I don't know if the angels actually considered my generous offer, but they went off and investigated the details with the CEO-at-the-time of my 'shorting'. That CEO clearly needed to have more employment law training in his MBA program and he also needed to watch Rashomon[62] a few times, because his view of what happened was a completely different reality from mine. To me it sounds delusional, so fortunately most of reality is confirmable on real pieces of paper. The CEO comes back with all kinds of "we agreed to this", "your benefit was working half time", "you could make it up elsewhere", and so on. Various other details came out, which I have already mentioned, like he had no means or intent on paying more than one year of my salary when we signed a four-year employment contract.

Because it appeared normal negotiations were not going to work, I looked up what my non-negotiation options were. In the past I assumed I would have to take the startup to court, and so I had never thought of looking up the details. The distraction to my main purpose in life of filling the aquarium would have been too great. But I was wrong. California cares quite a bit about *protecting employees.*

Within the office of the Labor Commissioner of the State of California, there is a Department of Industrial Relations, and within that department is a Division of Labor Standards Enforcement. And on the web site of that Division there is a three-page form. Three

---

[62] Akira Kurosawa: Rashomon. A movie retold from four different perspectives

very simple pages to file a Wage Claim. A Wage Claim that if understood and accepted by the Labor Commissioner, changes this battle from being between an *employee* and a company, to being between *California* and a company.

Nine • point three

Some bleeding did happen, but it was relatively minor. I could fix bugs in the source of Sencha Touch myself. And leverage another Javascript swiss-army-knife (jQuery), I could fix various other weird misbehaviors. We made the ASH deadline, and I went to Disneyworld!

There was actually little reason to have me in Florida. It is just one of these "make sure the developer is around in case of disaster" shows. Anything I could do from Palo Alto, I could do from Florida. All the servers were in Texas, so I just flipped the direction I was from them. But I do admit staying inside, and visiting Disneyworld. I think I got a hotel inside because I registered a little late (didn't realize I was going), and because… it was Disneyworld. I mostly worked in my Hotel on another Eveo project, but I did venture out into Disneyworld with my companion and picked up trinkets for my family.

My companion was a journey doll named Sirius. Katrina had made Sirius for school, and was happy to have him go to Disneyworld. A journey doll is a doll that is sent on a journey and is supposed to send back postcards and trinkets. Sending away a doll you made is a bit difficult for a child, but ideally you have great faith in people and send the doll through one adult and another as they wander around the world. Katrina wasn't quite so trusting to let total strangers take Sirius on trips, but she did let her family take the doll around.

Disney now has pins you can trade, and one night I was having dinner with my pin-laden journey doll, and a Disney employee traded a very special (employee only) pin for one of Sirius's purchasable pins. Sirius came back to Palo Alto with a couple steps up over my daughters ☺

Family: Atomic

When "western" people talk about atomic families, they generally mean just a married couple and their children. But that is not what I mean. I have my Koi, which matches that classic definition, but my atomic family are the people who are emotionally, geographically, and intellectually on my side. We share a common purpose, and are collocated enough to execute it together. I would like my parents to join my atomic family, but they chose to stay outside Philadelphia and far from my community. With that choice they have made it both geographically and purposefully impossible to be a part of my family. When Rebecca's brother joins us for marketing or brunch, he and his wife become part of my atomic family. A nephew visits: atomic. A close friend of my daughters' sleeps over: atomic. A coworker needs me: atomic. These various protons can come and go, but when they are near, they get fully bonded into our nucleus. If you are a part of my nucleus, I will do almost anything for you… as if you were my own. Because you are.

Nine • point four

After ASH, PeerCase shifted direction pretty rapidly. Although iPads were great for demonstration, it turned out that most doctors were still on PCs. And with PeerCase up and running, getting doctors signed up (business development) was far more important than product development. But the next six months still had a fair amount of work to build out a new PC-capable vs. touch UI.

The end of PeerCase for me occurred in the summer of 2011. Another CEO approached me about joining the cofounding team. This was supposed to be a AAA team building a AAA gaming company… all the 'A's sounded good since even if I am clearly an 'A' player by this point, alone I can't make a startup successful. PeerCase could have kept me if they had made some reasonable kind of equity offer. But Eveo and PeerCase just couldn't manage it. After weeks of requests, they made no offer at all.

Fini Nine

Right: Product

PeerCase was amongst my saddest startups. We had a good idea for a valuable product. Helping people survive and even thrive in spite of a major illness seemed quite valuable to humanity. Connecting patients to the best care seems quite valuable. The product was built well enough for it to be pleasant and effective to use, especially after it was available on both mobile and desktop devices. But having a good product is not sufficient. You must have paying customers, and in some markets that can take a huge amount of time or special connections. It appears that PeerCase had neither, so we built something good and useful but could not get customers before time ran out.

Wrong: Timeline

The timeline of a startup can be hard to identify when it launches. Both the timeline needed for customer and product development, and the timeline of funds and expenses. You can try to project the numbers, but they are almost always very optimistic. They are optimistic about how much funding the company will get. Optimistic about how long employees will work for equity vs. cash. Optimistic about how short it will take to build the product and find customers willing to pay for it. Optimism is very expensive.

From startup six onward, I very much became more and more of the realist within my startups. I would really build the product in stead of estimating how long it would take. Or if pressed, I would give realistic estimates of how long things would take, and then do my best to match or beat those estimates. I would realistically try to hire no one else, because each additional person is an expense and a source for distraction. These were all to make sure the startups timeline was better than expected.

PeerCase had a great timeline for the product, but the timeline for the company was unresolvable and in spite of investment offers to take the product forward into large customers, the original owners decided the offer was not good enough and simply shut PeerCase down.

Kindness: Laptop

Rebecca helps Palo Alto raise money for the public schools. You would think that any reasonable property tax on houses where each are guaranteed to be "some number of millions" would make raising educational money a frivolous task. But California has Propositions. And to the demise of the educational system from Kindergarten through Graduate School, Californians were idiotic enough to pass Proposition-13. And with one proposition, generations of children were "shorted". So now communities have to do additional fund-raising to try to make ends meet within their public schools

Rebecca has a coworker 'J' who lives in a similar situation as we do in Palo Alto. I don't know J or her family very well, but I can tell that they have an aquarium and it is draining water at a similar rate to ours. But this year, my ability to refill aquariums is at an all-time high: I am consulting for several large companies and getting my customary rate at all of them. I also know computers quite well, and can tell when a computer is "right" and "wrong" for a person.

One day I get a text from Rebecca asking about computers. It turns out that 'J' needs a new laptop: the current one is not working for her at all. She wants the new laptop to be an Apple, and is trying to figure out the *minimum* configuration that would possibly work. Rebecca and I converse a little bit about this, and then I simply stop responding.

The problem is that the *minimum* configuration for a laptop is not really a sensible concept. Or it should mean something very different than people interpret it. Laptop computers are not upgradeable. At least not easily or inexpensively. And although you can add peripherals to a laptop, that makes them much harder to transport and setup. So I ended the conversation when I had enough information to figure out what J needed for her minimum configuration. And because J was not planning on spending that much money, she was going to buy something that was sub-par to what she minimally needed. And in a few months would have been very unhappy.

An advantage of living in the heart of Silicon Valley is that computers are abundantly available. A short drive from my office and I was at the Apple University Avenue store. Another short drive and I was at J's office. And I quietly dropped off the *right* computer on her desk as a Mother's Day present.

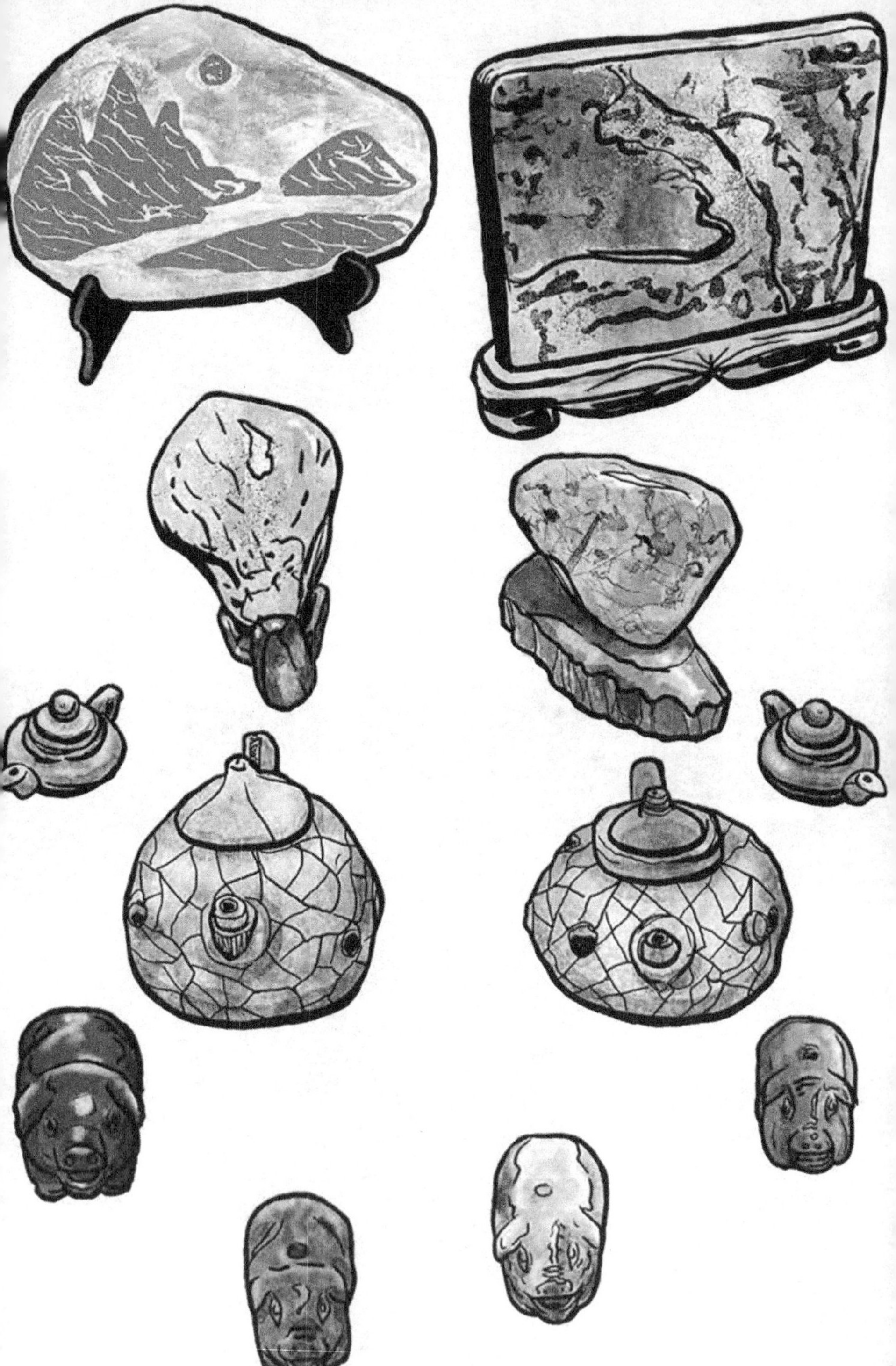

1300

TEN

The AAA gaming company was Rumble Games. I was one of five cofounders that went along with the founder/CEO to bootstrap this company. The play was impressive: we had a great art director, a great (if a bit intense) studio manager, a game designer, a game engineering lead, and a platform engineering lead. In startups, people get pompous titles that will only make sense once the startup succeeds. The platform engineering lead was really just a platform engineer (there was only one), and that person was me. My pompous title was Vice President, Platform Engineering.

I was very confident I was an 'A' player by this point. I was pretty sure the CEO was also an 'A' player: he had $2MM in the bank before hiring any cofounders, and he used that money and a lot of equity to get serious talent on board. The equity was especially generous: it was protected from dilution post Series-A funding.

Stock: Dilution Protection

Dilution protection is a seriously valuable thing. Consider the Rumble offer: say they offer me only 5%, but that 5% will be 'post-money' after Series-A. That is a serious offer, and much better than a 10% offer without that protection. If Series-A gives us $20MM, then I (on paper, and ignoring preferences) can now make at least $1MM over four years. And I don't really care what the pre-money valuation was at all, although it will raise things a bit. At $10MM pre-money, I now have $1.5MM on paper.

With the 10% and no protection, the company has to be valued at $10MM for me to get even the $1MM. Rumble was ultimately too generous on equity vs. cash for it to work out for me, but I do acknowledge the generosity of the equity offer.

Ten • point two

So I believe the CEO and I are 'A's. I can see the work of the art director, and compare him to the incredible FooMojo artists (from

ILM, Tippet, DreamWorks, etc.), and he clearly stands on gaming-oriented equal grounds. The studio head is *way intense.* That is not a problem for me: I really want startups to move along very rapidly and intensity helps. He and I collaborated on getting the Rumble site live: we effectively 'paired' in the right sense. I did everything IT related and he made sure things were really working. We sat together in the 'war room' of Rumble, which was called 'Kawar' for the Kick-ass-war-room. It was intense and effective. The site is beautiful and runs well.

So now we are up to four 'A's with a little bit of personality tensions. Unfortunately, adding in the last two cofounders did not add more 'A's. It added lots of problems. Gaming programmers are commonly not really the same ilk as 'software engineers'. Some of them are, but many of them love gaming more than they love learning how to build effective and reasonable quality software systems. Building effective and reasonable quality software systems requires a lot of candor about how good your software is. And if it is not good, it requires being open to learning from people who are highly skilled at building good software. Building a good game requires a lot of candor about how fun your game is. And if it is not fun, it requires being open to people who are highly skilled at building fun games. In my opinion, Rumble failed badly at these. But I will not harp on them. It was an interesting "play".

The team was definitely good for the money in startup terms. Within a couple months we had almost $17MM in the bank based on the founding teams' skills and early efforts. With that much money we should have had an incredibly long runway to investigate, build, pivot, investigate, build, pivot, and investigate yet again. But size matters, and Rumble is part of the "bigger is better" startup approach. I didn't agree and kept my team to two people (a trusted developer) until a third person was somewhat forced upon me. But Rumble as a whole grew to 50 people in 6 months, so however lean my team was, the burn rate of the company was enormous.

Palo Alto: Slumlords

You aren't intrinsically a "slumlord" by owning a slummy kind of

house in Palo Alto. The houses aren't *that bad* to intrinsically be a slum. For a landlord in Palo Alto to be a slumlord, they have to behave like a slumlord. And although we have lived in Palo Alto for many years, we have had only one slumlord so far. Unfortunately, it was our first.

But fortunately, my family is relatively immune to most of the negative aspects of slumlords.

In spite of our slumlord thinking we should travel back in time sixty years when we were home, we replaced a 1950s stove with something a bit more current. And replaced a noisy and ineffective dishwasher with something reasonably quiet. And replaced the energy-guzzling old refrigerator with a properly green one. All the showerheads became both water-saving and more effective. We removed all the drapes in the house because they were ratty and disgusting. Everything we did was reversible. The items we removed were placed into storage above and in front of the strange drop-in room in the garage. Things like the refrigerator were put in the garage too, in case the slumlords were going to be unreasonable on the value of the new one.

For many years, I was not even sure our landlords were slumlords. Maybe they just had exceedingly bad taste? Supposedly they had lived in this house for at least a few months, lived in the squalor, so maybe squalor was natural to them. When we suggested that the house needed to be painted before we moved in, they seemed to think that quite novel. Walls as grimy as the curtains just made sense. Having clean white walls was novel. The painter we hired did a great job, and the house looked and worked a lot better after we transformed it.

We had beaten back the power of the slumlords by simply "owning" the house: putting our own money into fixing what was wrong with it. I think other tenants would not have enough gumption to do that and would have been at the mercy of the slumlords. Or they would simply move out after they realized what was going on.

Ten • point three

Within a couple months we had good funding and what could have been a long runway. By eight months in, we had a beautiful web site, some impressive infrastructure for running and monetizing games, and a lot of beautiful artwork. Unfortunately, we had no actual game. We had three potential games, but none that was ready for broad release let alone making us any money.

The first was KingsRoad. By month eight, millions of dollars had gone into developing KingsRoad. The money had produced a very beautiful and thoroughly uninteresting game. Even worse, the part of KingsRoad that made it interesting was the *content* of the game. The story. Just like a book or movie. Putting a storyline into a game is much more expensive than into a book or even a movie. The game has to work. It has to not be too hard. It has to not be too easy. Content-based games are so expensive to build that they are basically guaranteed to lose money unless you can charge a hefty price for them. KingsRoad was free.

The second game was a fun little mobile game called Nightmare Guardians. You were a super-hero protecting a sleeping child from dangerous nightmares. It was a great concept that would seem to have Plants vs. Zombies appeal, but somehow the company never really invested in it.

The third game was a futuristic first-person shooter that could easily have done very well. First-person shooters have very high appeal to twenty and thirty year old males who have a lot of free time and discretionary income. Again, the company put minimal investment into it.

By eight months in Rumble had three games that are all behind schedule, lots of expenses every month, and requests for a lot more infrastructure. And a growing tension between me and a couple other cofounders.

Commitment • point two

To make good progress in learning anything requires commitment. If you just go through the motions, take some lessons, do a little practice, and repeat... you will not get anywhere significant. The human body and mind are miraculous learners, but only when you convince them that something is important. A couple hours a week does not convince your body or mind. Twenty hours a week and you have their full attention. You will learn because your body and mind think whatever needs twenty hours a week must be keeping you alive. Improve or perish.

I had progressed a bit on my serve, and in practice I was doing pretty well. But when I played matches, it fell apart. My toss would be wrong, my wrist snap would be missing, or I wouldn't commit to jump to hit a ball that is inside the court. I was basically stuck, or moving very slowly. All the rest of my game was fine, so this was the critical last piece to becoming decent. The only choice was to lean-in, and I started serving in the morning. And by morning, I mean the first time there is enough sunlight for you to hit a tennis ball. I was going out to serve at 5:30 or 6:00 AM. I am naturally a night owl, so this was serious commitment.

And by 'the morning', I mean *every* morning. In any given week there are seven mornings, and every week I did seven hours of serving. The benefit of picking the god awful time of 6AM is it does not interfere with your day. The marines have a slogan "We do more before 9AM than you do all day!" Well, I did more serves before 8AM than most tennis players serve all day.

A full serving workout was a total of 16 "overs". You take eight balls, and you serve them from one side, and when they are all "over" the net, you go to the other side and do the same thing back. This simulates game serving much better than a hopper of balls, and it has very little overhead. I wear a biking shirt that has three pockets in it, plus pants that have two, so in total, I can easily carry 11 balls (two balls in each of the five pockets, and one in the hand). I highly recommend biking shirts for tennis. Besides the extra pockets, they have some very nice designs.

So eight times sixteen is 128 balls, *if* all the balls go over in the first try. If a ball doesn't go over, it doesn't count and you eventually collect it and try again. When I was serving badly, 16 overs would probably mean more like 160 balls. In a doubles match, you probably serve around ten balls per service on average. And you only serve every fourth time. So this was equivalent to 64 games of doubles, or 32 games of singles. A five set match with tiebreakers could have a total of 65 games, but non-professionals tend to play at most three where needing the tiebreaker is rare. So the 160 balls are definitely more than most tennis players serve all day.

This extra commitment worked wonders. My serve started clicking, and became stable in matches. I was very happy to have pushed through the wall. So happy I still serve seven days a week, even though it doesn't seem like I need it. But I do: I want my body and mind to consider tennis a means of survival. I want to get better, forever.

Ten • point four

The tension among the management team was from several different aspects, but I can summarize it from my side into one simple phrase "I was at Rumble to win, and win as quickly as possible".

I do not know the details of the other cofounders, but in my case, I had given up more than a third of my salary to join Rumble. I was not wealthy, and my family had no other significant sources of income. When I gave up a third of my salary, I expected to run as quickly and perform as skillfully as I could possibly do for the next year. So I could get that third of my income back, and hopefully something more. Otherwise my family would be out on the street.

About month eight, it was clear the company was not on course to make that "we have something within a year" deadline. My family was running out of money. So I asked the CEO let me sell back half my stock in exchange for a more sustainable salary. He said no, and then went on to ask me about private schools for his daughter. A month later he said no again.

Employees: CLC • point two

It was like many anime in which the main character can transform into some crazy powerful entity when the odds are against them. It took me a while to learn how to transform: the three simple Wage Claim pages that must have made sense most people were talking in terms that mismatched with how I was actually paid. But ultimately I would understand the three pages, augment them with three more as supplemental details on a month-by-month basis, and finally my caseworker would be happy with me. The last call I had from her, she was making sure I was compensated fully for my unused vacation.

I didn't immediately file the Wage Claim. Before that, I tried to negotiate a bit more. I made two more offers, both less than what the Wage Claim ultimately entitled me to. One was interestingly fair: if I had negotiated to be half time with the startup, what would have been mutually beneficial and fair? I figured this out quite easily: with every startup I have a target salary I want, and they almost always pay me a little less. For this startup they paid me about three quarters what I 'target', so if instead they paid me half of my 'target' for half of my time, that seems fair. So I offer to make that the negotiation amount. It is a little higher than my original $60K estimate because they shorted me for a lot more months than I apparently cared to remember. But it seemed fair and saved them quite a bit of money.

That offer was again rejected, or at least nobody responded to it. After I filled out the Wage Claim I saw it had a "penalties" section, so before sending the Claim in, I made one last offer that if the startup just paid the amount calculated by the Wage Claim, they could avoid the penalty (which I thought may have doubled the number). Again, there was no response. I even offered to meet in person in case people wanted things to be off the record. I eat at a restaurant with Rebecca every Tuesday, and she was going to miss it this week. So if anyone wanted to talk with me, they just had to come to the restaurant, to talk over a free lunch. Nobody showed up.

Filling out the form gave a total of $85,284.09. About three times

my original offer. And if the penalty doubled it, that would be $170K. That would be a windfall of epic proportion for my Koi and me. It wouldn't be worth the pain that could have been saved four years earlier, but it is better than nothing.

Oh, and the really funny part to the whole story. Wage Claims have a statute of limitation. It is four years if you have a written contract. The first month the startup shorted me was April of 2010. The angels could have just left me alone, but instead they poked me "just in time". My Wage Claim had an office-received stamp date of April 30th, 2014. Ironic.

Ten • point five

I am slowly running out of money for my family, Rumble can't seem to build a viable game, and the game we have in production is incredibly demanding and bug-ridden. The number of features within the Rumble infrastructure was amazing. We could present at technical conferences with all the capabilities we had. But having a lot of capabilities does not make a company money. Only paying customers make the company money. And we basically had none of those. It was Velidom 2.0 with a lot more money. I had already done that once and didn't want to do it again.

During the Spring, the dynamic of me wanting to "go live", "get customers", and "be stable" collided with others wanting to keep iterating on features. A dynamic between a nine-startup veteran looking to win quickly (or go home) and others who clearly had a bigger picture that wanted to paint. Given I ran all the production servers almost 24x7, I was getting more and more stressed by the operational overhead for something that was not producing any significant income.

The cofounders had regular meetings where things would flare up. Sometimes it would happen in the main room as well, where one of the cofounders would start yelling at me and others. The situation was not good, but generally people went back to their desks and back to the work that needed to be done.

END? ELEVEN!

This book has failed many times. It's worse failing was it's ending. In spite of being extremely happy and optimistic, I had written a thoroughly depressing ending. Failing at the end of a book is far worse than failing early on. A reader has invested a lot of her time listening to my thoughts, and then I let her down. I don't tell her "how to be ecstatically happy", which was the original subtitle. I don't tell her how to do "Succeed in life through relentless failure", which may be the current subtitle. She is disappointed by my "almost unreadable vanity project"[64].

Fortunately for you, I think the version you are reading is much better than any version before it. And a big part of that improvement is due to some very constructive feedback from earlier readers. The book was first published (by me and also Amazon) in the summer of 2014, and since then many helpful people have read it and given feedback. You can see their names listed in the credits, and the book you are reading is much better for it. Especially the ending. I hope you enjoy it.

Eleven

Putting my life into ten startups was extremely draining. After Rumble Games, I had called it quits and shifted back into consulting for software development and patents. The work was relatively interesting, but in many ways unfulfilling. As a consultant, you are not building much of anything. Instead you are helping other people learn to build things, and then let them have at it themselves. One summer day, my "leave" was dramatically halted and Eleven was born. Two of my biggest projects ended in the same week and I had a lot of free time on my hands. So I played a lot more tennis. Started looking for more projects. And was thoroughly bored. Boredom is very powerful, and made my 'vigilant' for something to end my boredom.

---

[64] A not particularly constructive piece of feedback by an early reader "F"

a DP sitting in front of the multi-million-dollar house you do not own, or the transformative power of freely (even recklessly) giving away your time and your money to others, will help you. Or you own interesting and bizarre equivalents. Then you just need to ponder the universe a bit more. You need to ask yourself "why can't I understand?" and "what are my boxes?"

I have for a long time been interested and amazed by Zen Buddhism. I have pondered "one hand clapping"… read up on motorcycle maintenance, and later (with kids) pleasantly read the line "Hi ku!"[69]. I think all these readings and ponderings have impacted my life, but they did not radically transform me. My transformation was not a slow evolution. It may have needed a lifetime of evolution for me to survive what happened and pick the particular exit I picked. But my transformation was explosive and effective.

It all started one summer. I would lose a job, a house, almost all my possessions, and the world would add several perils beyond these three. All within the span of a month. At the end of it, all the perils had been dispatched successfully, but it required me to "unlock" every box I have ever placed myself into. I stepped out of them all. And after stepping out of all these boxes, I would only put back a couple constraints that I cherished. After this happened, many people started calling me insane. My wife and children. Friends of many years. Likely some strangers (that I love) who pondered why I spent an hour driving to their store, just to *thank them.* Thank them wholeheartedly. And then simply leave.

I am different. That is more than okay, I believe it is awesome.

Eleven • point three

As I finish this book PortaPlanter is in a limited beta through Kickstarter. By the time you read it, that Kickstarter will be closed and some number of people will have signed up to try the product. If that is successful, I will go to local retailers and try to sell some more. And from there, I may go on Shark Tank or otherwise seek

---

[69] Zen Ties

expansion capital. PortaPlanter is the best distillation of how to do a startup right that I tangibly know. Ten failures and one maybe success. Even if PortaPlanter doesn't succeed, it was not a financial burden to my family, was an interesting problem to solve for me, and touched a lot of my community. I can't say that PortaPlanter will succeed, but it is off to a very good start.

Entreprendre Eleven

Love: Readers

Some of my readers paid nothing for this book. That is because these particular readers gave me much more than the retail price of the book. They read my book, gave me feedback, and helped me tailor the book: to be more informative and more readable *for you.* These readers read a version of my book before it was finished. This I will call my Minimal Viable Book. It was the book you are reading, a couple generations earlier. It was younger, but you could tell where it was headed. It was a teenager looking to become a valuable adult: an adult that would positively contribute to the community.

But my MVB was unsure; as was I. Were we really on the right path to benefit the community? Could we do better? Were we going to make irreparable mistakes? One of the great things about a community: it can easily answer these questions. If only you ask. And so I asked.

Back in June, a year or so ago, I gave away copies of my MVB in exchange for my communities' and friends' and colleagues' and total strangers' time. My MVB was possibly worthless, so I certainly could not charge anything for it. And these peoples time was of great worth, but haggling over the value of that was going to be too complicated to be viable. So I gave each of them my MVB and simply asked them to help me.

I asked each of these people to give me *personal editing* of my MVB. Tell me what you think, as a reader, of this book. Do you like it? How could I better speak to you? Did I say anything confusing? I paid professional editors to look for grammar, tone,

and spelling issues. I was not asking people to do something for free that I could get from others for money. In asking people for their *personal editing,* I was asking people to do something for me, for free, that I could only get from them. If they were my audience (which they were), how could I make them happier?

Again in June, a year or so again, I believed had completed my minimal viable book. And so I wandered Palo Alto giving my MVB out to the community...

With the help of my communities, my friends, my colleagues, and total strangers, the book you have in your hands is now a TVB: a truly viable book. Or at least I think it is. I thank all the people who gave my MVB their personal and professional editing. And I thank you for reading what all of our efforts produced.

Success: Love

Early readers were concerned I would not deliver on my subtitle: "How to succeed through relentless failure". I hope I have shown you relentless failure by now, and if you have read everything else above, you might think I consider myself an abject failure. That I do, but at the same time a tremendously successful person. I have a family that is amazing and that I love dearly. I have a far-reaching community that is very special and that I love. I do work that I love and am proud of. I try to succeed, and I relentlessly fail, but I don't completely fail. And by not completely failing, I succeed a little at a time. Relentlessly failing is the same as relentlessly succeeding. So the subtitle was the answer to the question it posed. It was its own answer: "You succeed through relentless failure". It just took a few pages to explain it.

Kindness: End!

Over the two years it has taken to write this book, I transformed and it transformed. The book was never meant to be a biography or a vanity project. If it was either of those, I would have simply shelved it. It was meant to sell a million copies and help a good percentage

ABOUT THE AUTHOR

Mark L. Fussell lives with his wife Rebecca, and two daughters Maya and Katrina, in Palo Alto, California. After surviving ten failed startups, Mark is consulting to make ends meet. Oh and doing startup number eleven:

- PortaPlanter.com – Healthier, easier, and greener plants!

During the rest of his time, he:

- Teaches kids robotics – see PaloBots.com
- Plays and teaches a lot of tennis – see SuperSonicFox.com
- Mentors kids in startups – see FaceLick.com
- Helps schools – see Ohlone.pausd.org, GirlsMS.org, NuevaSchool.org, Crittenden.mvwsd.org
- Mentors kids in programming and other quests
- Helps small businesses with their IT and technology needs
- Spends a lot of time with his family

All of these things, Mark does for free, because after ends meet, you don't really need more money. So why not make things easy and just give yourself?

Oh, and Mark wrote this book (see SlumsOfPaloAlto.com). He hopes you enjoy it.

Made in the USA
Monee, IL
04 November 2026

67374640R00115